As a physician practicing internal medicine, I know how prevalent stress is in the lives of most individuals. The book is clearly written and is filled with concrete suggestions which can be put to immediate use to help prevent or control stressful situations. It is a very practical manual which I recommend to the general public.

J. M. KIELY, MD
Mayo Clinic

A fresh approach to managing stress—A constant companion to all working women.

CAROLYN B. ELMAN, EXECUTIVE DIRECTOR
American Business Women's Association

A sparkling example of a professional program for getting the job done. It certainly worked for us.

LINDA K. PAGE, DIRECTOR
State of Ohio Department of Commerce

Barbara Braham's new book CALM DOWN at last considers total lifestyle as she helps us deal with stress. Exploring the link between diet, attitude, exercise and responsibility, Barbara outlines a clear and intelligent approach to add both meaning and years to one's life. And, she understands the magic of making it fun.

RICHARD C. MIZER, PRESIDENT
Century Bank

Ms. Braham has captured an area which is very much needed but has been neglected; the unique stresses of the work place. Her holistic approach provides the reader with many coping skills for becoming and remaining psychologically healthy.

FIONA TRAVIS, Ph.D.
Columbus Psychological Center

CALM DOWN

How to Manage Stress at Work

The Scott, Foresman Applications
in Management Series

<hr>

ROBERT B. NELSON, *Editor*

CALM DOWN

How to Manage
Stress at Work

Barbara J. Braham

SCOTT, FORESMAN AND COMPANY
Glenview, Illinois   London

Grateful acknowledgement is made to the American
Business Women's Association for permission to reprint
SMART Goals excerpt from *Chapter Goal Setting and
Planning*, copyright 1989.

Library of Congress Cataloging-in-Publication Data

Braham, Barbara J.
   Calm down: how to manage stress at work / Barbara J.
Braham.
      p.   cm. — (The Scott, Foresman applications in
management series)
     Includes bibliographical references.
     ISBN 0-673-46089-4
     1. Job stress. I. Title. II. Series
     HF5548.85.B69   1990
     650'.01'9—dc20   89-10765
                                  CIP

1 2 3 4 5 6 KPF 94 93 92 91 90 89

ISBN 0-673-46089-4

Scott, Foresman professional books are available for bulk
sales at quantity discounts. For information, please
contact Marketing Manager, Professional Books Group,
Scott, Foresman and Company, 1900 East Lake Avenue,
Glenview, IL 60025.

For RICK,
who loves me even when
I forget to practice
what I preach

Series Foreword

The Scott, Foresman Applications in Management Series provides short, practical, easy-to-read books about basic business skills.

Low on theory and high on practical techniques and examples, this series addresses the key skill areas needed to be a successful manager in business today. It supplies specific answers to questions you have and offers new approaches to problems you face in your job.

Each book in the series is written by one or more individuals who have extensive first-hand experience on the topic being discussed. The drafted books are then reviewed by several front-line managers to assure that each meets their needs in delivering practical, useful information in a format that is easy to understand and use.

I am confident that this book—and others in the AIM series—will provide you with tips and techniques to enable you to do your job better today and in the future.

Robert B. Nelson
Series Editor

Acknowledgments

Thanks to Rick Sullivan for his unending support and encouragement, insightful comments on the manuscript, and for the wonderful graphics; Marilyn Frankel for her support and feedback on the manuscript; Mary Struble, a biofeedback and stress management consultant, for her thoughtful comments on the manuscript; Tonie Feil, Dick Mizer, Brian Braham, Kris Miles, Beverly Williams, Jackie Pauley, Bill Bickham, Craig Stanley, and Ben Willard for their insights into corporate stress; Judy Latshaw and Allyn Erhardt for research assistance; Robert Nelson for his valuable editorial suggestions; Amy Davis for her guidance in the publishing process; and the thousands of people who have taken my stress management workshops and shared their lives with me.

Contents

PART III

APPLY THE MODEL

CALM DOWN

How to Manage Stress at Work

Part I

EXPLORING STRESS

1

Assess Your Stress

"**C**alm down," he said. "If you don't, you may not come out of the next one alive."

Sure, that's easy for him to say, Allan thought as he lay in bed recovering from a sudden heart attack. He'd been trying to do that for months, but it wasn't working. How can you expect a guy to "calm down" when he has to deal with irate customers, constant deadlines, an impossible boss, and demands to do more, more, more?

No matter what kind of stress you face in your life, there are ways you can calm down. This book will show you how.

WHAT CAUSES WORK STRESS?

Stress can be caused by just about anything: deadlines, traffic, public speaking, the boss, meetings, organizational change, and so on. Ask any number of people what causes them stress and each will give you a different list, because each of us perceives stress differently. All causes of stress can be grouped into five major categories.

Desired Changes at Work

These are things you usually anticipate with excitement; you look forward to these changes. For example, a new project, a move to a new location, retirement, and a promotion are all things you might perceive as positive. Although that doesn't make them less stressful, it does change your *attitude* about the stress. As you plan for these changes, you will probably feel invigorated and excited. In fact, you usually choose these stressors in your life! Because you choose them and generally view them as positive and exciting, desired changes at work rarely are the reason you seek "stress management" information.

Unexpected Changes at Work

Unlike desired changes, unanticipated changes are usually negative and sometimes devastating. A reorganization, a new boss, a lost customer, new government regulations, and marketplace changes are all examples of unexpected, unplanned changes. Such situations create acute, short-term stress. Because of their dramatic nature, you usually turn to colleagues, friends, and family for support. Therefore, despite their intensity, the changes do not usually create long-term stress management problems.

Exceptions to this occur if the change is kept secret or if you have no emotional support. For example, knowledge of a pending down-sizing or reorganization that you cannot discuss creates more stress than if you could talk openly about it.

"Sneaking" Stress

This is a major source of stress for most of us and perhaps is a key reason you sought out this book. "Sneaking" stressors are the little things that add up, the "straw that breaks the camel's back." Consider the morning you oversleep, burn the toast, discover you're out of coffee, and hit every red light on the way to the office! Does this sound familiar? After a couple of these days, you discover you are feeling stressed. The stress doesn't result from any one major event, as with desired or unexpected changes. Rather, it results from a series of small stressors that sneak up on you, until one morning you awaken with some symptom.

This kind of stress is not resolved quickly. It continues day after day and week after week, wearing you down just as surely as water running over a rock eventually wears it away.

Take, for example, the cases of Jerry and Mildred. Both of them are suffering from "sneaking" chronic stress, although for different reasons.

Jerry has worked for the same manufacturing company for the past seven years as a purchasing agent. He enjoyed the work until about a year ago, when he got a new boss. Now it seems he just can't do anything that pleases this man. For everything he does right, his boss criticizes three other things. Jerry has tried to talk with him, but they just don't seem to communicate. Now Jerry hates to see the boss coming and feels tired and irritable at the end of the day. Just the thought of Monday mornings has started to make him feel depressed on Sunday afternoons.

Mildred works in the accounting department of a small chemical company and is also under chronic stress. Eighteen months ago her company was bought out by a larger, multinational corporation. Since then, her firm has been in constant turmoil. First there was uncertainty about who would be laid off. Then the new management arrived, with their own ideas about how to do things. The accounting procedures have changed four times since the buy out! There seems to be no stability anymore, and she wonders how much longer she can cope with the situation.

Both Jerry and Mildred are beginning to experience the effects of chronic stress, which, over a prolonged period of time, sneaks up on us in the form of symptoms. Rather than a specific incident, it is the buildup of small demands that results in chronic stress. You may not realize how deeply the stress is affecting you until you suddenly are faced with a symptom such as fatigue like Jerry's or Sunday depressions.

Ask yourself these questions to see if you have "sneaking" stress.

1. Do you feel tired much of the time, even after a good night's rest?

2. Have you felt less positive about life recently, as though things don't seem to work out in your favor?

3. Do you notice yourself feeling irritable much of the time?

4. Do you notice yourself feeling frustrated much of the time?

5. Does it seem harder and harder to get started on important assignments each day?

6. Do you sometimes wonder when someone will notice that lately you haven't been as productive as you usually are?

7. Do you notice that, although you aren't sick, you don't really feel well?

The more "yes" answers you give to the above questions, the more likely that stress is starting to sneak up on you. If this is the case, you will find the life change techniques in this book especially helpful.

Self-Imposed Stress

Each of us would like to believe the stress we experience is coming from the "outside": our jobs, the people we work with, the economy, and so on. Although these outside events may serve as triggers, the stress actually originates on the "inside." In other words, we do it to ourselves.

Are you a worrier? If so, you're creating your own stress. You find ways to upset yourself. There is always something to worry about. Will there be an accident on the way to work? Is your work "good enough"? What do other people think about you? Will you meet the deadline? The list goes on. None of these situations need be stressful, but worrying about them makes them so.

Perhaps you are a workaholic, routinely working over 60 hours per week. You arrive at work before the sun rises and stay long after dark. You feel some guilt about the number of times you've let family and friends down by promising to attend some function and then arriving late or not at all. You probably have a sinking feeling that no matter how hard you work or how many hours you put in, you keep falling farther and farther behind.

How well do you manage your time? Do you routinely schedule more into your day than you realistically can accomplish? Do you find yourself habitually late because you tried to squeeze in "just one more thing"? You may be aware that you are doing this to yourself, yet you don't seem to be able to break the pattern.

On the other hand, maybe you are a negative thinker. You want things to work out for the best, but you can't help but see the potential problems. You try to be cautious and consequently see only the worst in other people. Your life may be filled with fears—from fear of failure to fear of success.

These and other traits cluster together to form a personality that feels stress in even the most relaxed situations. In reality, it is not outside events, but how we interpret these events that causes stress for us. The good news is that self-imposed stress is 100 percent within your control!

Physical Environment Stress

Although there are many different stressors, we don't usually think of the physical environment as one of them. Thus, you may have overlooked it as the cause of your symptoms. That's what happened to Chuck, who worked in the data entry department of a large direct mail company.

Chuck just couldn't understand why he was having so much lower back pain. He couldn't recall any injury to the back. He bought a new mattress, and that didn't help. He talked to friends who suggested it was stress. That didn't make sense to him, though, because he loved his work and his marriage was terrific. After taking over-the-counter medications for several months, he decided to seek medical advice. The culprit was identified quickly. Chuck worked at a desktop computer all day, and the chair was the cause of the problem. Added to that was the intensity with which Chuck worked, often hours at a time without even a stretch break. A new chair and regular breaks solved the problem.

Let's look at another example—a woman who worked in the collections department of the Attorney General's office.

For the past two weeks, Aisha had been coming home irritable and edgy. Usually delighted to see the children, she had been short-tempered and easily upset, constantly yelling at them to "Be quiet!" "Stop all that noise!" and "Go play in the other room!" It wasn't until after she and her husband talked that she realized how much the construction near her office had affected her. The sound of jack hammers had been nearly constant for two weeks. Aisha had to yell to talk to coworkers, and she had difficulty concentrating. When she left the office, she craved quiet and solitude.

Noise and uncomfortable furniture are just two environmental stressors. A smoke-filled office can cause headaches; air pollution of any type can cause irritability or physical complaints; and intense heat or extreme cold can affect your mood and energy.

Common Work Stressors

Take a moment now to jot down the kind of stressors you experience at work.

Desired work changes _____

Unexpected work changes _____

Sneaking stressors _____

Self-imposed stressors _____

Physical environment stressors _____

You might want to know if the stresses *you* experience are common to others. The most frequently cited causes of job stress are: time pressures (deadlines and scheduling); inadequate support; interpersonal conflict with a boss or subordinate; fear of failure; unclear expectations; and change.

The next section will give you an opportunity to complete a questionnaire to assess your current level of work stress.

Braham's Work Stress Inventory

Figure 1.1 is an instrument that lets you see the relative severity of your work stress. Take a moment now to look through this list and put a check mark beside any situation you have experienced in the past year. A check mark beside any of the items in Section A indicates sneaking stress. The severity of your stress is based on how long you have been in this situation. Remember that these chronic stressors are the most difficult to manage. For the items in Section B, a total of ten or more checks indicates high work stress, a total of five to nine checks indicates moderate work stress, and a total of five or fewer checks indicates low work stress.

The greater the number of checks, the higher your risk for experiencing symptoms associated with the

FIGURE 1.1   Braham's Work Stress Inventory

Check any of the following experiences you have had in the last 12 months.

Section A

_____   Fired
_____   Laid off
_____   Quit without another job
_____   Company reorganization (buy out or
                merger)

_____ Company experienced major growth
(doubled in size)
_____ On-going conflict with boss
_____ On-going conflict with peers
_____ On-going conflict with subordinates
_____ Company lost major client or source of
funding

_____ TOTAL

Section B

_____ Major disappointment (not selected for
promotion, project not funded or
cancelled, etc.)
_____ No room for advancement
_____ Highly political environment
_____ Fired an employee
_____ Laid off an employee
_____ Multiple bosses
_____ No control over daily work schedule
_____ Bored at work
_____ Changed bosses
_____ Manage multiple projects
_____ Give speeches/presentations to higher
levels of management
_____ Promoted
_____ Demoted
_____ Received a negative performance
appraisal
_____ Gave a negative performance appraisal
_____ Transferred
_____ Travel regularly (8 + days per month)
_____ Made a major wrong decision
_____ Change in senior management
_____ Job description changed

_____ Company moved
_____ Work overtime regularly
_____ Unclear expectations
_____ Face frequent (daily or weekly)
            deadlines
_____ Cyclical heavy workload (budgets, tax
            season, etc.)
_____ Changing priorities
_____ New technology
_____ Regular customer contact
_____ Company lost money over past year
_____ Major change in your industry
            (government regulations, competition,
            etc.)

_____ TOTAL

---

stress. By practicing the ideas in this book to CALM down, you can manage those stressors and make them work for you.

UNDERSTANDING STRESS

Now that you know what causes work stress—just about anything—let's define exactly what you're dealing with. Hans Seyle, a pioneer in stress research, defined stress as "the non-specific response of the body to any demand."[1] As we have just seen, that demand can be desired, unexpected, sneaking, self-imposed, or environmental. Why is it, then, that one person feels stress in a particular situation while another person feels completely relaxed?

The Role of Perception

Bill is the Director of Finance at a large lawn-care company. He is often asked to make presentations to senior management and the Board of Directors. Whenever one of these presentations is scheduled, he starts to worry about it. He has always felt uncomfortable in front of groups, and even though he is prepared, he sometimes goes "blank" in the middle of his talk. Because of his fear, he often rushes through his presentation and notices later he left out a key point. His boss has told him that he could advance further in the company if he would develop his presentation skills. So far Bill hasn't wanted to take any classes or do anything that requires him to do any more speaking than he already does.

Brian, on the other hand, loves to speak. He is the Director of Franchises for the company that employs Bill. Brian has always been a bit of a "ham" and loves to be in front of a group. He speaks easily from a brief outline and welcomes the opportunity to get in front of a group whenever he can. He likes to tease Bill, because Brian can't understand what is so scary about giving a speech.

In any situation, some people will see a threat and feel stressed, while others will see opportunity and feel excited. Bill feels threatened about speaking, whereas Brian feels challenged. Situations in and of themselves are neutral; how you perceive them affects how you feel. In Chapter 3 we will take an in-depth look at how you can control stress through thinking and perception. For now, we want to expand our understanding of stress to include the importance of perception. Let's say that stress is the nonspecific response of the body to any demand *you perceive as a threat.*

Control versus Controlling

One of the most critical areas of perception is *control.* Do you believe you have control of your life? The more you feel in control of what happens to you, the healthier you will be. People who feel they have control of their lives, their jobs, their time, and so on experience less stress than people who don't feel in control. This is why some low-level employees feel more stress than senior management. While it is true that senior managers have greater responsibility and make more frequent and far-reaching decisions, they also are more in control of their schedules, the projects they work on, and the kind of help they will use. In contrast, first-line supervisors do what they are told by management, respond to the needs of their employees, make few decisions, and often have their days controlled by someone else's schedule. A receptionist can't even go to the bathroom when she wants to—she has to wait for coverage! According to the National Institute for Occupational Safety and Health, among the most stressful jobs are licensed practical nurse, quality control inspector, public relations specialist, computer programmer, and bank teller—all positions in which employees don't feel in charge of their jobs.

An important distinction needs to be made between "having control" and "being controlling."

The latter is a negative behavior used most often by people who feel they do not have control. They want things done their way and on their schedule. Thus, a payroll clerk who feels she doesn't have much control over her work becomes controlling with other employees. She might establish an arbitrary rule that payroll sheets must be turned in by 10:00 A.M. on Wednesday. If a sheet is turned in one minute late, she refuses to process it.

The greater your own sense of control, the more powerful you feel. Ironically, this leads to less controlling behavior. If you believe you can handle a situation, you don't need to make it happen your way. You are free to relax and respond to whatever occurs.

Sometimes we have no control over situations. However, people who feel they have control of their lives realize we always have control over our *responses* to the situations. It is this belief that buoys some of us, while others sink in exactly the same situations.

Sometimes we give away our control. For example, if we are asked to volunteer for an extra project, rather than say "no," thereby controlling our own time, we reluctantly agree and complain to others, "I had no choice." This giving away of our control results in double stress: first, the lack of control, and second, the time pressure.

One theme that runs throughout this book is the importance of maintaining control whenever you can, of the situation, if possible, and of your response to the situation, if not.

Eustress and Distress

Not all stress is bad. Most of us need a certain amount of stress to feel motivated. Who hasn't said he or she works well under pressure? In fact, insufficient stress is stressful! Think back to a time when you felt bored in your job—not challenged or stimulated. Remember how the time used to drag? If you think about it, you probably will recall feeling stress.

As you can see in Figure 1.2, *dis*tress comes when we are underloaded or overloaded with stress. *Eu*stress occurs when we have enough stress to feel motivated and challenged and to work at peak productivity. This chart depicts the Firehouse Syndrome. Fire fighters are either sitting in the firehouse waiting for something to happen or racing to a fire: underload or overload. People such as accountants, retailers, and construction workers are especially prone to the Firehouse Syndrome because of the cyclical nature of their jobs (tax season, holidays, warm weather). Anyone faced with seasonal or cyclical work confronts this problem.

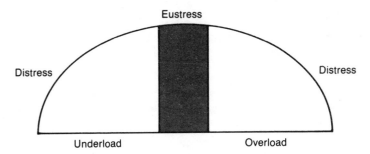

FIGURE 1.2   The Firehouse Syndrome

Fight-or-Flight Response

When the body has a demand placed on it or perceives a threat, it responds physically with the *fight-or-flight response.* This served human beings well long ago when they encountered physical threats, like wild tigers, that they had to run from or fight. Today when we need to call a dissatisfied customer on the phone, our bodies react with the same fight-or-flight response. Unfortunately, this is not a situation in which we can fight or run away. Instead, we need to deal calmly with customers. Our bodies, not knowing this, proceed with the fight-or-flight response anyway.

Once a threat is perceived, an alarm goes off throughout the body. The heart rate increases, blood pressure goes up, breathing rate increases, and blood is drawn away from the extremities and concentrated in the deep muscle groups. Also, the pupils dilate, the jaw clenches, and adrenaline, sugar, and fats pour into the bloodstream. These mechanisms work well when one is in a life-threatening situation; however, when one needs to return a customer's phone call, activation of the fight-or-flight response will wear out the body unnecessarily.

It's a little like driving your car. If you continually drive with the emergency brake on, you never will have the power or speed of which your car is capable. After a while, you will burn out your brakes. It is equally possible to "burn out" your body.

Nearly 75 percent of all illness is believed to be caused or worsened by unmanaged stress. When one is under strss, the immune system is suppressed, thus increasing vulnerability to illness. At the Indianapolis 500, the race cars make a pit stop after about forty laps. All the tires are replaced, the radiator is cleaned, the suspension is adjusted, and the car is refueled. When the race is over, the entire engine is replaced. Although many of us drive our bodies like race cars, it is not so easy to schedule a "pit stop" during which the heart is replaced, the muscles are repaired, or the stomach is relined! In the next section we will look at wear and tear on the body.

SYMPTOMS OF STRESS

When we don't manage our stress, our bodies experience the fight-or-flight response over and over, and we begin to experience symptoms. Just what those symptoms will be varies from person to person. Each of us has "weak links," vulnerable places that tend to break down when we are exposed to repeated stress. We may be affected in any one or some combination of the following ways.

Physical Symptoms

It's when our bodies develop symptoms that we decide to take action to reduce stess. In 1986, $458.2 billion was spent on health care, and much of that was a direct result of unmanaged stress.

Look over the list below, and check off any physical symptoms you are experiencing.

_____ Headaches
_____ Sleep disorders (e.g., insomnia, oversleeping, early morning awakening)
_____ Backaches (especially lower back pain)
_____ Clenching the jaws or grinding the teeth
_____ Constipation

_____ Diarrhea and colitis
_____ Skin rashes
_____ Muscle aches (especially neck and shoulders)
_____ Indigestion or ulcers
_____ Hypertension or heart attack
_____ Excessive perspiration
_____ Appetite change
_____ Fatigue or loss of energy
_____ Increase in accidents
_____ _____ (Add your own)

Emotional Symptoms

These are the symptoms that may lead you to a counselor's office. Check off the symptoms that you experience.

_____ Anxiety or worry
_____ Depression or crying easily
_____ Mood swings
_____ Irritability
_____ Nervousness
_____ Lowered self-esteem or feelings of insecurity
_____ Increased sensitivity or feeling easily hurt
_____ Angry outbursts
_____ Aggression or hostility
_____ Feeling emotionally drained or burned out
_____ _____ (Add your own)

Intellectual Symptoms

In the following example, you will see the impact stress can have on intellectual functioning.

Carol couldn't understand what was wrong with Karen. Always an excellent worker, this past week had been a disaster. As Office Manager, Karen was responsible for a variety of tasks that Carol had stopped monitoring long ago. Suddenly Carol found herself involved. The bank deposit wasn't added properly, and there was a call from the bank. The Federal Express packages destined for locations across the country all had the same address on them. A grant that had to be copied in triplicate and sent to three different agencies had pages missing. Karen began to seek Carol's advice on routine decisions she had always made. Worst of all, when Carol talked to Karen, she was faced with a blank stare that left her wondering if Karen really was listening.

Karen was experiencing personal problems, and try as she might to leave them at home, they came to work with her. In her case, the stress showed up in the office as intellectual symptoms.

Look at the list below and check any symptoms you have.

_____ Trouble concentrating
_____ Difficulty making decisions
_____ Forgetfulness
_____ Confusion
_____ Poor memory and recall
_____ Excessive daydreaming
_____ Preoccupation with a single thought or idea
_____ Loss of sense of humor
_____ Decreased productivity
_____ Lower quality of work
_____ Increased number of errors
_____ _____ (Add your own)

Interpersonal Symptoms

Stress also can affect your relationships with others, both on the job and at home. Strained work relationships quickly can become one of the chronic stressors we identified earlier in this chapter. Now, in addition to the original stressor—perhaps changing technology in the office—there is the compounding factor of an unpleasant interpersonal situation. It is unlikely you'll get support to cope with the original stress if you damage your relationships with those who could support you.

Look through the list below and check off any symptoms you are experiencing.

_____ Inappropriate distrust of others
_____ Blaming others
_____ Missing appointments or cancelling them on short notice
_____ Fault finding and verbal attacking
_____ Overly defensive attitude
_____ Giving others the "silent treatment"
_____ _____ (Add your own)

The more items you have checked on the previous four lists, the more important the ideas in this book will be to you.

The first step in gaining control of stress is awareness. Until you notice when and how stress affects you, you cannot manage it. Look back over the symptom lists you have just completed. How does stress affect you? Can you recognize the early warning signals, or do you wait for symptoms? How intense are your symptoms? How often do they appear? As you become more attuned to your personal stress response, you can apply the CALM model more effectively.

THE CALM MODEL

The remainder of this book outlines a four-step process called the CALM model, which can help you manage the work stress you experience. Each step will show you ways to take control of your life so that stress works *for* you and not *against* you.

Don't Be Deceived by a "Short-Term Fix"

There is a big difference between *managing* stress and *coping with* stress. When you manage stress, you make it work for you; that is eustress. You can use the skills outlined in this book to monitor your stress level so stress does not become distress. You will learn to use your sense of control to take charge of stressful situations and your reactions to them. Most stress management efforts are long-term solutions to the stressors we experience.

In contrast, when you cope with stress, you're applying a "short-term fix." You look for ways to make the immediate pain go away without necessarily looking for ways to resolve the underlying causes. Unfortunately, many of the short-term solutions (*copers*), turn into long-term stressors. For example, if you use alcohol to unwind from a stressful day, you may feel an immediate sense of relief. However, if that coper is used continually, it can become another problem—alcoholism. On the other hand, if you choose to manage your stress, you'll use an exercise program instead of alcohol to relax and unwind. This long-term strategy builds your resistance to stress, and doesn't just hide it.

There are times when we all have used short-term solutions like drugs, alcohol, a warm bath, a shopping spree, fault finding, taking a day off, blaming, eating, smoking, or denial. However, if this is the only way we handle stress our health and our relationships are bound to suffer.

There is a better solution than short-term fixes: to *manage* stress and CALM down.

The Model

CALM down is a four-step process you can apply to any stressor you're experiencing, even if it is personal rather than work-related. It is a simple, easy-to-understand model that anyone can use. It is also a long-term stress management plan. The only difficult thing is making the commitment to implement it.

Look at the model in Figure 1.3. The first step, C, is to change the situation when you can. Chapter 2 explains the questions you can ask yourself to see if change is possible, then gives you several skills you can use to implement the change.

Chapter 3 describes the second step, A; accept the things you cannot change. There are situations we cannot control. Learn how to accept them without anger and how to keep your thinking positive.

The third step, L, is to let go. Chapter 4 gives you some suggestions on how to let go of your unrealis-

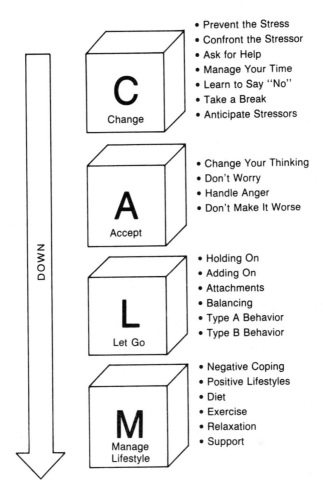

FIGURE 1.3 The Calm Model

tic expectations and negative belief systems. You'll also discover ways to let go of the self-imposed stress that only makes matters worse.

Finally, Chapter 5 will cover the fourth step, M; manage your lifestyle . . . and make it fun! This step gives you a number of ways in which you can start raising your resistance to tomorrow's stressors *today,* through exercise, diet, relaxation and emotional support.

The last five chapters of the book will apply the model to some common work stressors, including career change, difficult coworkers, working with computers, travel, and organizational change.

SUMMARY

Stress can be caused by desired or unexpected changes, sneaking stressors, our own attitudes and beliefs, or the physical environment.

Whether we experience a particular situation as stressful or not is determined by our perception of the situation. If we are overloaded or underloaded with stress, we are likely to develop symptoms. These may show up physically, emotionally, interpersonally, intellectually, or in some combination of these.

There is something we can do about stress. We can learn to CALM down by applying the model in this book.

REFERENCE

1. Hans Seyle, *The Stress of Life,* rev. ed. (New York, New York: McGraw-Hill, 1976), 1.

Part II

CALM DOWN: THE MODEL

2

The C of CALM: Change the Situation

Most of us become aware of stress when it is acute. Our muscles tense, we experience some of the symptoms discussed in Chapter 1, or we feel anxious. At this point the typical response is to try to cope with the stress.

PREVENT THE STRESS

There is a better first step. Before you jump into coping with the situation, stop and allow yourself a few minutes to think. Take several deep breaths to relax and clear your mind. Then ask yourself this question:

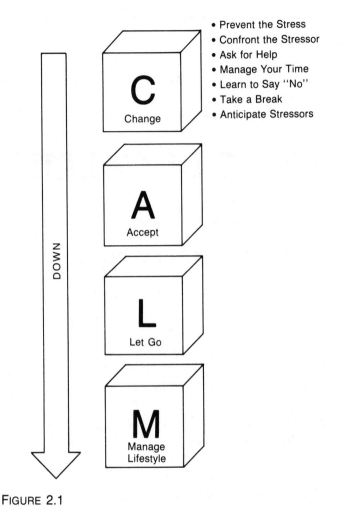

- Prevent the Stress
- Confront the Stressor
- Ask for Help
- Manage Your Time
- Learn to Say ''No''
- Take a Break
- Anticipate Stressors

FIGURE 2.1

''Is there anything I can do to change the situation to avoid or reduce the stress I am feeling?''

It may help to have a piece of paper handy so you can write down any ideas that come to mind. Then after you list all your ideas you can go back through the list and decide which of them, if any, are workable. This brief "time-out" lets you brainstorm strategies to manage the stress, rather than just coping with it.

The process also gives you a sense of control. No longer powerless or helpless against the stress, you are now actively deciding the best way to respond. Too often we give away our power at this early stage and then feel victimized.

Let's look at the case of Jerome, who works in the accounting department of a hospital.

Jerome felt overwhelmed. He had a major budget review due at 4:00 P.M. He had been working on the project for the past week and still had about 4 hours of work in front of him. The problem was, he didn't have 4 hours available. He had a supervisory conference scheduled in the morning and a committee meeting scheduled in the afternoon. He coped by skipping lunch and taking some of his work to the committee meeting. The meetings usually didn't demand his full attention anyway.

Jerome did not take the time to think through his situation. Instead he *reacted,* and in the process increased his level of stress. If he had used the CALM model, he first would have asked himself some questions like those that follow.

Can Someone Else Do It?

Who else can help? Is there anyone who could attend the meeting for him? Could anyone else finish the budget review for him? Could part of the budget review be done by someone else, thereby reducing the time Jerome would need to spend on it?

This is a question you can ask yourself when you start to feel stressed. Who else can help you? Is there someone in your department who could give a helping hand? Or is there someone in another department in the company with a lower workload who might be able to help you? Sometimes it can be more cost-effective and less stressful to hire a temporary worker to assist with a special project. You may be able to use a temporary worker to handle the routine tasks while you focus on the special project.

Can Something Be Delayed?

Jerome assumed everything had to be done at once. He created more stress for himself by trying to attend a meeting and work on his report at the same time. Most of us are less productive when we try to do two things, each of which requires our full attention, at the same time. Jerome would have been wiser to think through the consequences of changing one of his deadlines. For example, could the budget review be delayed until the next morning? Could the supervisory conference be rescheduled for another day? Could the meeting be postponed? In Jerome's case, it is reasonable to assume he could delay the supervisory conference. This would give him at least 1 extra hour.

Can I Substitute Anything Else?

Jerome might ask if he could submit a draft of his budget review rather than the final report. Perhaps he could give an overview with a final detailed written report to follow. Instead of attending the committee meeting, he might prepare a brief written summary of his opinions or suggestions and deliver these to the committee chair along with how he would like to vote on any known issues.

Is It Essential?

What is the worst thing that could happen if Jerome doesn't do everything? How important is the committee meeting? Is it essential? Would it make much difference if he called and said he could not attend? What about the supervisory conference? If this is a weekly meeting, would it matter if he cancelled, or is this the Annual Performance Appraisal, which cannot be delayed? Who is the budget review for? What are the consequences if it is not complete? Is this a report to the Senior Vice President, or is this a progress report to his immediate supervisor?

Will a Job Aid Help?

Another question to consider is, "Can I use any tools or training to help me do the job faster or more easily?" Suppose Jerome was manually preparing for his budget several scenarios based on various percentages for salary increases. If he were using a spreadsheet program like Lotus®, it would automatically make these calculations. Learning a new job aid might be more expensive and time-consuming in the short run than doing the calculations manually. However, if this is a task Jerome completes often, the long-term gains may exceed the short-term costs. To plunge ahead without thinking about this can keep Jerome perpetually stressed. By asking yourself this question, you may identify ways to reduce future stress, even though you cannot change the current stress.

Can the Stress Be Avoided?

All these questions help us address the stress associated with a project, but what if the source of stress is a person or a situation? In that case, ask yourself all the previous questions and one more: Can the stressful situation or person be avoided entirely? Imagine that you fight rush-hour traffic every morning and evening getting to and from work. You may cope with this now by trying to relax while you drive or perhaps by listening to audio cassettes. Using the CALM model, your first step is to evaluate the situation and ask yourself if the stress can be avoided. One solution might be leaving the house earlier, before the rush hour begins. You also might discuss with your boss the possibility of flex time, so you could come in earlier or later to avoid the rush. In addition, you could consider public transportation. Any of these choices puts you in control and simultaneously lets you minimize the stress.

What if your boss is the source of the stress? The two of you simply don't get along, and whenever you are together you feel knots in your stomach. Can you avoid the situation? It's possible. You could request a transfer to another department or work on projects that give you independence and minimal contact with the boss. In a company with multiple shifts, you might change your hours. And as a last option, you can quit. It is not necessary to "make yourself sick" by staying in a negative situation. Recognizing your choices gives you more control. If you elect to stay and deal with the stressful relationship, you have minimized your stress simply by being in control of the decision. Then you do not feel stuck, trapped, or helpless. You have *chosen* to stay in the situation.

It is important to make a distinction here between *ignoring* a situation and actively avoiding it. Ignoring it is a passive and powerless response. It is like burying your head in the sand, hoping that when you look up the stress will have disappeared magically. This is just what it sounds like—magical thinking— and it leaves you feeling less in control and more stressed. Ignoring stressors does not make them go away.

In contrast, avoidance is an *active* strategy in which the stressor is not hidden from view, but actually removed from your situation.

Can the Situation Be Confronted?

If you cannot avoid the situation, then ask yourself, "Can I reduce the stress by confronting the situation or person?" Imagine again that you are in conflict with your boss. You may not want to leave the situation because you love the job and enjoy working with your colleagues. Before you decide to accept the situation the way it is and simply cope with it, use the CALM method. Why not confront the specific problems you have with your boss and attempt to resolve them? If you can resolve the differences, you may reduce or eliminate the stress. In the following pages we will discuss the skills you can use to confront a person or situation.

The power of these questions is that they help you recognize your current situation and face squarely what you like and don't like about it. Then you can take charge of how you will respond to it.

After asking yourself these questions, you will have a list of possibilities before you. Let's look at Jerome's options to reduce his stress:

Don't attend the meeting—send someone else.
Don't attend the meeting—cancel.
Postpone the supervisory conference.
Cancel the supervisory conference.
Negotiate a later deadline for the budget review.
Submit a less comprehensive budget review than originally planned.

By combining several options from his list, it would be possible for Jerome to meet the 4:00 P.M. deadline without unnecessary stress.

How often do you try to do everything, like Jerome did, with the result that you feel "stressed out"? Remember that, once you are aware of feeling stress, the first step in managing it is to change the situation whenever you can.

Take a moment now to jot down a stressful situation you are facing. Then ask yourself the CALM questions.

Situation: _____

_____

_____

Can someone else do it? _____

_____

Can it be delayed? _____

_____

Can I substitute something else? _____

_____

Does it have to be done? _____

_____

Will a job aid help? _____

_____

Can the stress be avoided? _____

_____

Can the situation/person be confronted? _____

_____

Action I will take: _____

_____

CONFRONT THE STRESSOR

Deciding to change the situation is not enough to make it different. You also will need the skills to take the actions you have chosen. The remainder of this chapter tells you how to develop the skills you need to manage stressful situations.

How to Confront Another Person

Most of us feel uncomfortable when we think about confronting another person. This is because we don't have the tools to do this graciously and effectively. In fact, for some, confronting the situation would create more stress than merely coping with it. Part of your strategy will be to assess whether it is wiser for you to cope with a situation or confront it.

Confrontation is a lot like removing a splinter from your finger. It is painful for a few minutes, but once you remove the splinter, you feel better. Looking back on it, taking the splinter out wasn't so bad, especially compared with the benefits.

Some people fear that confrontation will damage or add distance to a relationship. Here's a way to confront and still keep the other person "near and dear."

D—Describe the situation.
E—Express your feelings.
A—Ask for what you need.
R—Reinforce the other person.[1]

Describe the Situation   In this step, you want to be as objective and succinct as possible. This is not the time to list fourteen reasons you are upset with someone. Unfortunately, this often is what happens, because we fail to confront each other with our small concerns. Instead, we wait until we have collected a laundry list of complaints, which we "dump" all at once. This makes us feel better because we got it off our chests. However, it does not resolve the situation, because the other person usually feels blamed, attacked, or "dumped on" and is not willing to work toward any changes.

If you do have several concerns, focus on one and let the others wait for another time. This will en-

1. Thanks to Mary Struble for the DEAR acronym.

able you and the other party to stick to the issue. With one issue rather than several, the chances that the other party will become defensive are reduced.

If you can explain how the situation is creating stress for you, the other party will be more able to understand things from your perspective. Remember when we discussed the role of perception in stress (Chapter 1)? The fact that you are experiencing conflict with someone is an indication that each of you perceives the situation in a different way. Once you can stand in each other's shoes, it is much easier to resolve the situation. If you fail to help other people see your point of view, they can only remain locked in their points of view. The goal here is for both persons to expand their points of view and reach a "viewing point."

An analogy will help explain this concept. If you've ever been to the mountains, you know you can stand on the ground, look up, and see a mountain peak. Think of this as your point of view. From this point of view it appears there is only one mountain—the one before you. If you hike up that mountain, though, or take a tram to the top, an amazing thing happens. As you look out from the summit, you suddenly realize there are many, many more mountains (or points of view), none of which you could see previously. This is what you want to achieve with the other person—the ability of each of you to see the other's point of view.

Express Your Feelings After you describe the situation, identify how you are feeling. You might feel upset, frustrated, disappointed, confused, nervous, scared, or anything else. Once you know how you feel, begin your confrontation message with, "I feel _____ (feeling word)." By starting out this way, you minimize any chance that the other person will become defensive. Too often, confrontations are begun with the word "you." Is it any surprise that the other person instantly feels defensive and stops listening?

When you begin with "I," you are describing how you feel in the situation, and you are assuming responsibility for those feelings. There is no blame inherent in this statement. When you begin with "you," an invisible pointing finger seems to accompany your words, and that finger is pointing at the other person, blaming them and holding them accountable for the situation.

Ask for What You Need After describing the situation and expressing your feelings, make a suggestion as to how the situation can be changed. If you don't ask for what you want to be different, how can anyone know to make a change? This isn't because they are being stubborn or resistant; they may not have thought of the same solution that you have in mind.

Reinforce the Other Person Don't forget to acknowledge the other person! This can be as simple as saying, "Thanks for your consideration," "Thanks for your help," or "I appreciate your cooperation." If the other person actually makes a change, give them specific reinforcement for that change. For example, "I notice you aren't smoking during our meetings anymore. Thank you." This reinforcement will maintain the change you want, and make your next confrontation easier.

Let's see how these steps would look in an example situation. Mike works in the employment services department in a state government agency. He is responsible for compensation and benefits, and during the interview process provides candidates with a salary range for the position they've applied for. Mike feels frustrated and angry because his boss does not use the same salary figures and often hires candidates at above the agreed-upon entry-level salary. Then Mike has to find a way to justify it in the files. He fears that some long-term employees will find out about this practice and file a grievance. Mike now feels stressed and apathetic whenever he meets with candidates, because he anticipates the boss will change whatever salary figures he offers.

After analyzing his situation, Mike decided he wanted to confront his boss about this situation. He felt if he could get this changed he would feel good about his job again. This is how he decided to approach the boss.

"Fran, we've had several situations lately in which a candidate tells me you quoted a higher salary than I offered in the initial screening. I feel embarrassed when this happens. And it creates problems for me when I prepare the new employee file and need to justify a starting salary that is above our policy guidelines. This practice makes us vulnerable to a grievance, or even a law suit. In the future, would you talk with me before you offer a candidate a higher starting salary, so I can advise you as to whether or not we can support the higher figure if challenged? I appreciate your cooperation."

You can use these same steps when you need to confront someone. You will not want to confront every source of stress. This process requires some thoughtful planning and usually creates some short-term stress of its own. However, if you are experiencing chronic stress with an individual or a situation, then confrontation is an excellent strategy for maintaining a sense of control and managing the stress.

ASK FOR HELP

When you are in a stress-producing situation, it is easy to take on the role of "Super-Human." You expect yourself to be able to do everything and handle everything without help. It's as though asking for help signals that you are incompetent and not able to do the job yourself. This unwillingness to ask or fear of asking for help is also connected to the wish to have things done "my way." To allow anyone else to assist is to risk that the job won't be done exactly as we would do it. Both these attitudes are outmoded and highly ineffective when it comes to managing stress.

So, how do you go about asking for help? Anticipate as far in advance as possible situations that may be stressful. Imagine that you have a proposal that should be postmarked on a particular day 3 weeks from now. This is a complex bid which will require the input of many people. On the day the proposal is due you are scheduled to go out of town. Begin thinking right now about the last minute tasks that may need to be done, and begin to alert people. In this way, they can leave some gaps in their schedules to accommodate your needs. For example, tell your secretary about the project now, so he or she can take care of routine tasks in advance of the deadline. Notify the messenger that you will need the proposal hand-delivered to the post office on that day. Alert other managers to the potential need for secretarial assistance to prepare final graphs and charts. Check with the copy room employees to be certain they can duplicate your proposal when it becomes necessary. Lining up this kind of support in advance reduces the crisis-management mentality that is responsible for so much stress. It is also far easier to ask for help in advance than it is to ask moments before a deadline.

When you do ask for help, think about who can best help you. Try to identify several possible resources, so that if one person turns you down you have an alternative. Specify exactly what you need from them and why. This allows them to give you honest answers about whether or not they can help. If they understand the why, it increases motivation to follow through on the commitment. Tell them when you will need their help. This way, you can confirm their availability, and they can make necessary arrangements. If you know, also tell them for how long you will need their help.

With this degree of clarity, there are no surprises on anyone's part. Too often we are asked to help out, we agree, and then we find out the task is more complex or time-consuming than we thought. This leads to resentment and an unwillingness to be a future resource. Be careful not to abuse your supporters, or you may find yourself working alone!

A simple format you can use is, "Here's my situation . . . and what I need is. . . ." Once you have expressed your need, the other person can respond with a yes, a no, or a compromise.

Asking for and giving help is a two-way street. Don't expect that others will help you again and again if you don't return the favor from time to time. In fact, helping others whenever you can becomes a good policy, because you build a bank account of helpfulness that you can cash in on when you face a stressful situation.

STEPS TO ASK FOR HELP

1. Put aside the need to be Super-Human and the need to have something done "your way."
2. Select the best person to help.
3. Ask for help by explaining your situation, specifying what needs to be done and why, and estimating how long it will take.
4. Get a commitment and let your helpers do what they agreed to do.
5. Express your appreciation.

MANAGE YOUR TIME

After negative thinking, the inability to manage time is the second greatest cause of self-imposed stress. Poor time management results in crisis management, which results in stress.

One of the first time problems people run into is not scheduling enough of it for a task. Then they experience stress because they can't get the task done in the available time. Remember Jerome from the beginning of this chapter? He had a budget to prepare and on the final day found himself running short of time. Part of his problem may have been not allowing enough time to complete the project. This can be tricky, because Parkinson was right when he said work expands to fill the time available. So, how do you realistically "guesstimate" time needed for projects?

Two techniques work. One is called a Time Log, and the other is called a Project Log. Both will require some time up front. Look at this as an investment that will pay big dividends rather than spending or wasting your time.

Time Log

A Time Log is a record you keep over a period of 1 to 2 weeks in which you record as accurately as possible what you do during the day. In Figure 2.2, you can see that the day has been broken into 15-minute segments. This is the smallest unit of time most people will need to monitor. You may find it more useful to keep the Log in 30- or 60-minute intervals. Make this determination on the basis of how you typically spend your time. For example, if you are a social worker who sees clients every hour, it may be more realistic for you to keep a Time Log with longer time intervals.

Next, develop some codes to represent your most common activities. You will use these codes to save you the time of writing out repetitive and long descriptions when you keep the Log. For example, your codes might include:

FIGURE 2.2   Time Log

	Activity		Activity
7:00 A.M.		12:45 P.M.	
7:15 A.M.		1:00 P.M.	
7:30 A.M.		1:15 P.M.	
7:45 A.M.		1:30 P.M.	
8:00 A.M.		1:45 P.M.	
8:15 A.M.		2:00 P.M.	
8:30 A.M.		2:15 P.M.	
8:45 A.M.		2:30 P.M.	
9:00 A.M.		2:45 P.M.	
9:15 A.M.		3:00 P.M.	
9:30 A.M.		3:15 P.M.	
9:45 A.M.		3:30 P.M.	
10:00 A.M.		3:45 P.M.	
10:15 A.M.		4:00 P.M.	
10:30 A.M.		4:15 P.M.	
10:45 A.M.		4:30 P.M.	
11:00 A.M.		4:45 P.M.	
11:15 A.M.		5:00 P.M.	
11:30 A.M.		5:15 P.M.	
11:45 A.M.		5:30 P.M.	
Noon		5:45 P.M.	
12:15 P.M.		6:00 P.M.	
12:30 P.M.		6:15 P.M.	
		6:30 P.M.	

T   = Telephone call
M   = Meeting
S   = Supervisory conference
R   = Reading
I   = Interview
RW = Report writing
LW = Letter writing
TR = Travel time
C   = Chitchat, socializing
E   = Eating, coffee break
B   = Brain work, thinking

Add to this list any codes that would represent major activities you perform. You can further refine this by adding numbers to it. Let's say you spend an hour making marketing calls. You could record this on your Time Log as T-8, which would tell you it took 1 hour to make eight calls. The particular system you design for tracking your activities is less important than maintaining an accurate record of what you do with your time.

After you have data from a week or two, you can analyze your Time Log. This is your moment of truth! As you look at your Time Log, you are collecting data on two important aspects of your time. First, where is your time going? Is half of it spent on the phone? How much of your time is being spent in meetings? How much time is "lost" to coffee breaks and chitchat? (Be honest with yourself.) How much of your time was spent working on your highest priorities? If you had a major project due, is that where you spent your time, or did your time get eaten up by lower-priority tasks? The more willing you are to be truthful with yourself as you re-

view your Time Log, the more powerful the learning
can be. No one else need see this; it is for your personal use.

The second stage of analysis is to review your key
activities and see just how long they took. If you
were preparing your monthly report, how long did
that task take—1 hour, 15 minutes, 2 hours? How
about travel time between appointments—is it taking a couple of hours per week or as much as a couple of days' worth of time? If you were orienting
a new employee, how much time actually was spent
in that process—was it a couple of hours a week or
a couple of hours a day?

Collecting this information will help you in two
ways. First, you will begin to develop a sense of how
long a task takes, which will allow you to plan your
time more effectively. Let's take the example of a
monthly report. You typically have allowed yourself 30 minutes to put it together before you send
it off to be typed. Now, as you review your Time
Log, you see that you actually spent 1½ hours. There
wasn't anything unusual about this month's report,
and you realize that you probably have been spending about three times as long as you thought on this
task. With such concrete data, you can ask yourself
how to streamline the process so it only requires 30
minutes. You also might recognize that this task war-
rants that much time, and in the future you will allow 1½ hours. If, as you review your Time Log, you
see repeatedly that you have estimated less time than
a task actually takes, you are identifying what may
be one of your major stressors.

Second, you will gain a better understanding of
how much flexibility you have in your daily or
weekly schedule after you study your Time Log.

Most people make one strategic error when they are planning their daily schedules. They plan as if they have 8 hours to work with. Most of us do not have 8 hours. That 8-hour day can shrink to 6, 5, or 3 hours, depending on our *usual and customary* activities. If your department has a daily update meeting that takes 15 minutes, you have only 7 hours and 45 minutes available to schedule. If you discover from your Time Log that you spend at least 1 hour every day responding to incoming phone calls, you're now down to 6 hours and 45 minutes. Continue studying your Time Log for routine expenditures of time that are part of your job and subtract them from your working hours. (Note that 30 minutes spent reading the paper, socializing, and drinking coffee every morning is not part of your job. That is wasted time that you need to reclaim.) Once you've done this, you know *realistically* how much time you have available each day to schedule for your high-priority work. If you've been scheduling 8 hours' worth of projects when you really have had only 6 hours and 45 minutes available, you have been creating stress for yourself and probably have been working long hours or taking work home on a regular basis.

The Time Log is such a valuable tool that you will want to use it to check up on yourself at least once a year.

Project Log

The second tool that can be invaluable to you in your planning is a Project Log (Figure 2.3). Large or complex projects may not be completed in the period

FIGURE 2.3   Project Log

Project: _____

Date Assigned: _____

Estimated Time: _____   Actual Time: _____

Date	Activity	Time (Hours)

during which you keep your Time Log. In fact, some projects can take several months to complete. A Project Log allows you to track the various components of a project and the time it takes to complete them. This is valuable for many reasons. If you are in a business such as an accounting or consulting firm, in which you are paid for a particular project, you need to know how long you spend on a project or you may underbid it. Without a Project Log, there is no accurate way at the conclusion of a task to evaluate whether you made money, lost money, or broke even. Even internal projects have a cost-benefit ratio that needs to be assessed.

In one management information system department, a monthly report was submitted to senior management by Marta. When Marta was on disability leave, Helen prepared the report. Helen decided to track how long it took her to prepare the report and discovered it was 5 hours! When she submitted the report to her Vice President, she attached a note asking if the report was worth the 5 hours of staff time needed every month to prepare the data. The answer she received was "no." Her decision to track her time and provide senior management with that information saved the department 5 hours every month—that's 1½ weeks over the course of a year.

You also can benefit from the Project Log for projects that are completed on an annual basis. Fred was responsible for the Annual Meeting at his company. This involved many tasks, including preparation of the Annual Report, mailing invitations, selecting guest speakers, arranging for a facility, and ordering meals and decorations. By keeping a careful project log, he was able in subsequent years to make a realistic schedule for each of the tasks, reduce his stress, and produce a more successful event.

In successive years, using the Project Log as a basis, you can continue to refine the project, finding ways to save time and even money. When you're promoted and need to delegate this task to a new person, you will have an excellent tool for monitoring progress on the project.

The Time Log and the Project Log provide you with benchmarks against which you can plan and measure your progress, like an athlete who establishes a baseline performance, then begins the process of looking for ways to be better and faster. Do not try to be *efficient* until you know you are *effective*.

Set Goals

Knowing where you are through the Time Log and Project Log allows you to think about where you want to be. To do this, you will need goals. If your company does not set goals (by means of Management by Objective or some other format), you can set them for yourself. Goals are the magic key to prioritizing your time and getting the important things done. Without them, you likely will be very busy, but a year from now you'll be in essentially the same place as you are now. A goal works like a magnetic force—it pulls you toward it. The more powerful the goal and the stronger your desire, the greater the pull and the more likely that you will reach it successfully.

You can set a goal for anything: sales, customer service, profits, turnover, growth, new products,

and so on. Just be sure your goals are SMART. A
SMART goal meets these criteria:

S —Specific
M—Measurable
A —Achievable
R —Realistic
T —Timebound

Specific What exactly are you going to do?
Quantify your goal. It doesn't matter how you quantify, just as long as it is clear and specific.

Measurable How will you know you have
achieved the goal? Remember to have in place whatever record keeping procedures you will need. A
goal can be measurable before the measurement
devices are in place. If they aren't ready to go, the
result is the same as not being able to measure the
goal.

For example, your goal may be to reduce customer
complaints. However, you don't currently keep
track of complaints. How will you know if you
achieve your goal if you don't have mechanisms in
place to measure it?

Achievable Can it be done? Is it possible? Have
others done it before you?

Realistic Being achievable is not enough. The
goal also needs to be realistic. You want it to be a
stretch—that will increase your motivation. If it is

unrealistic, though, it will become demotivating. Take into consideration what you have done in the past to be more realistic.

Timebound Set deadlines for your goals. Without deadlines, you have only dreams, empty words on a piece of paper. Deadlines might coincide with company time cycles such as fiscal year end, performance appraisal, or calendar year or some other cycle unique to your company. Communicate these deadlines to others so you all are working toward the same deadline. Schedule regular progress checks so you know where you stand against your expected deadlines. This is especially important for long-range goals that may require months or even years to complete.

Don't overwhelm yourself with goals; keep a limit of three or four. Put the goals in a place where you can see them easily. Then, when you are faced with several tasks demanding your attention, look at your goals and ask yourself, "Which one of these activities will bring me closer to my goals?" That is the one to do.

This kind of strategic time management will result in more promotions than randomly doing everything that comes across your desk. Think about some of the people who have advanced in your company. They are probably people who have worked successfully on a few key projects, not people who have completed dozens of less valuable projects. If you focus your efforts on activities that move you toward your goals, you can't help but be successful, and you will experience less stress in the process.

Get Organized

- If your manager calls and asks for last week's sales figures and you can't find them on your desk, you will feel stress.
- If you fail to put a meeting on your schedule, and while you're writing a report a colleague walks by and says, "Hey, I'll walk to the meeting with you," you're going to feel stress.
- If your secretary gives you a letter to sign and it gets "lost," you have created stress not only for yourself, but also for your secretary.
- If one of your staff members asked for approval on her vacation and you "haven't gotten around to it yet," you have created stress for her.

Do any of these situations sound familiar to you? If they do, you need to get organized! In the first three situations you feel stress; in the last two, your lack of organization creates stress not only for yourself, but for others too. Read on for some quick, easy ways to get organized.

Keep a Clean Desk No matter what anyone tells you, if the desk isn't clear of all papers except the ones you are working on, you can't be as organized as when it is clear. Take the time to go through what is on it today, and either file or throw away all that paper. Set up baskets for your incoming work and outgoing work. Create a file for things you need to read. Develop a coding system to separate those items that need immediate attention, such as correspondence, from those that can wait.

Keep a Daily Schedule Carry it with you so that if a meeting or appointment is scheduled, you can record it immediately. Use it to jot down notes to yourself about things you need to remember. For example, if you have a meeting scheduled, you might make a note to yourself to bring a copy of the last meeting's minutes. If you are meeting with someone outside the company, you might write down their phone number.

Keep Frequently Used Information Handy If you are working on four projects, keep those files easily accessible so you don't need to shuffle through your filing cabinet for them. Make a list of frequently used phone numbers and keep it near the phone. Get a wall chart for scheduling multiple projects, so you can glance up and see what needs to be done and where you are against the deadline. Keep important customer information in a readily accessible form, whether on address cards or a printout. If you routinely find yourself looking up information, you probably need to maintain it in some more accessible form.

Use a "To Do" List Every day make a list of things that need to be done. Then, prioritize them against your goals. If something new comes up during the day, look at your list and ask yourself which task is most important. Once you have made your list, start with the most important things first. Try to give yourself a time "guesstimate" for the task and then stick with it. You can do more with a timeframe than without it. This is essential when you are managing multiple priorities. If you don't schedule some time each day or week for every project, you may find yourself unable to meet deadlines. Once you begin to manage your time more effectively, your stress will decrease. These ideas and techniques can help you change the situation you are in to give you more control, and thereby less stress.

MANAGE YOUR TIME

1. Periodically keep a Time Log.
2. Routinely maintain Project Logs.
3. Develop SMART goals.
4. Get organized! Keep your desk clean, maintain a daily schedule, keep frequently used information handy, and use a To Do list.

LEARN TO SAY "NO"

Too many of us operate under the Myth of Obligation. We believe that if someone makes a request of us, we are obligated to say "yes." Therefore, we feel we do not have the right to say "no." If we do, we suffer from feelings of guilt.

We forget that if a person asks a question, they are prepared for a "yes" or a "no." If they want only a "yes," they will make a statement, not a request.

There are five steps you can follow when refusing a request. First, notice how you feel when the request is made. Often you will notice a sinking feeling in your stomach because you do not want to do something. This an early warning signal that you need to refuse the request.

Second, ask questions. How often have you agreed to something, and later, when you found out what you agreed to, regretted your decision? Before you agree to something, make sure you know what you are agreeing to do.

Third, after you have collected information about both your feelings and the content of the request, decide. Don't be rushed! If you need to think it over, do so. If someone pressures you for a decision before you have time to consider it, refuse. If your decision is to decline, say "no." That two-letter word can be very powerful. Less specific phrases, such as "I'm not sure," usually turn into "yes."

Fourth, avoid excuses and explain when it's appropriate. We use excuses when we want to say "no," thinking they will soften our refusal. Often an excuse turns into a "yes" because the other party comes back with a solution to your problem (excuse). Rather than use an excuse, if you have an explanation, give it. An explanation says you would if you could, but you can't. It is not necessary to go into great detail with an explanation. For example, imagine you are asked to work late for the third time this week. You want to be with your family, and you know you need a break from the work. Rather than make an excuse, you can say "I have another commitment tonight." This is honest yet precludes a long, drawn-out explanation.

Fifth, stick to your original explanation, even if the other person persists in the request. This is known as the *broken-record technique.* You do this calmly and without getting upset.

HOW TO SAY "NO"
1. How do I feel about the request? Do I want to do it?
2. Ask questions. Know what you're being asked to do.
3. Say "no" if that's your decision.
4. Explain, don't use an excuse.
5. Use the broken-record technique, if necessary.

TAKE A BREAK

Sometimes the simplest way to manage stress is to get away from the situation for a little while. That "little while" may be 5 minutes, or it may be a 2-week vacation.

More research into the functioning of the brain is being done all the time. We now understand that there are two hemispheres, the left and right, which perform different tasks. The left hemisphere is responsible for language and rational and linear thinking. It likes numbers and order. The right hemisphere is the creative, problem-solving side. It operates more intuitively and sees wholes rather than parts. We need both sides. However, many of us rely heavily on the left side in our work and spend many hours concentrating on a task or problem. Research shows that the left brain needs little "stretch breaks" about every hour. We actually will be more productive if we stop and shift hemispheres than if we try to push ourselves as if we were running an endurance race.

What does this mean for you? Every hour you need to rest your left brain for a few minutes. Stop and take a few deep breaths. Spend a minute looking out your window, if you have one. Get up and walk to the drinking fountain. Let your brain relax for a moment. Please note that this is not a suggestion to take a 15-minute coffee break, go smoke a cigarette, or gossip with others in the office. It is a brief shift of focus for your brain and body.

If you are doing desk work, this is a great time to stretch your muscles. Stand up and reach for the sky, then bend over and touch your toes. Roll your shoulders, and relax your neck muscles. Then go back to work. If you work at a video display terminal, these exercises are essential; they will be covered in more depth in Chapter 8.

If you doubt the power of these minibreaks, think of a time when you were trying to solve a problem, but try as you might, you could not come up with an answer. Then, while you were driving home, taking a walk, or taking a shower, the answer came to you as an "Aha" out of the blue. The answer came when you turned the problem over to your right brain. You can facilitate those Ahas by giving yourself brief time-outs on a regular basis.

You also need longer breaks from your work, in the form of weekends and vacations. These are opportunities for you to recharge yourself. Many people have felt ready to quit a job, but after a week or two away returned refreshed, relaxed, and highly productive.

When we work for extended periods of time without breaks, we begin to lose perspective. Disagreements and disappointments get out of proportion. We take trivial matters too seriously.

If you've been priding yourself on how hard you work and how long it has been since you took a vacation, you are courting burnout. Another surprise—you may not be as effective as you think you are! When you do take a break, make sure it is just that. No work while you're on vacation! No calling the office every day or having the office call you. None of us is indispensable. To pretend that we are is destructive to ourselves and to the others around us.

Breaks will help you maintain balance, which is critical for managing stress. The harder you're working, the greater the demands, the more pressing the deadlines . . . and the more you need to stop and breathe and to take a break.

TAKE A BREAK

1. Give yourself minivacations about once an hour.
2. Use your vacation time!
3. When you're extra busy, *shorten* breaks—don't eliminate them.

ANTICIPATE STRESSORS AND PREPARE FOR THEM

We can anticipate many of the stressors we experience, such as preparing an annual budget, quarterly reports, or performance appraisals. When you know a stressor is upcoming, you can make some plans in advance to reduce its impact. Use all the suggestions in the preceding section on planning. In addition, here are other ways you can prepare for an anticipated stressor:

1. Don't take on any new projects that will demand a lot of your time or come due during the time of the expected stressor.

2. Take care of as much routine work in advance of the stressful time as possible.

3. Alert others about your stressful time, and advise them you will not be able to take on additional projects during that time.

4. Build in a reward for yourself (for example, take a vacation as soon as the project is complete).

5. Tell your family and friends about the stressful time and ask for their support and understanding.

6. During the stressful time, schedule some getaways for yourself to help you keep your perspective. These might include a weekend away, a regular night out, or any activity engaging enough to help you set work aside for a few hours.

7. Eat nutritious foods and get some exercise.

8. Be ruthless with your time. Do not take on any commitments that will increase your stress level. Say "no" graciously and regularly. Know

your goals and priorities and keep them upper-
most in your mind.

SUMMARY

The first step to help you CALM down is to change
the situation when you can. Start by giving yourself
some time to take a deep breath and think for a few
moments before you plunge into coping with the situation. If you can, manage the stress. To change the
situation, you will need to ask yourself the CALM-
ing questions: Can the stress be avoided? Can the
stressor be confronted? Does the job have to be
done? Is the job essential? Can someone else do it?
Can it be delayed? Can something else be substituted?
If you answer "yes" to any of these questions, use
the following skills to make changes: confront the
situation, ask for help, manage your time, say "no,"
take a break, and prepare for expected stressors.

In the next chapter, learn what you can do if you
can't change the situation.

3

The *A* of CALM: Accept What Can't Be Changed

There are situations that you cannot control and cannot change despite your best efforts. Some examples include a merger or buy out, a boss with personal problems, certain deadlines, new management, new government regulations, foreign competition, the weather, and other people's behavior. If you persist in trying to control these situations, you only create more stress for yourself. What can you do so you are not powerless in these situations?

You can accept them for what they are. Acceptance is not the same thing as giving up. Acceptance is a *choice* you make that puts you back in control. When you accept a situation, you participate in an active process, not a passive one. You make a conscious decision to move past judgement or past being angry and upset to face the reality before you. This

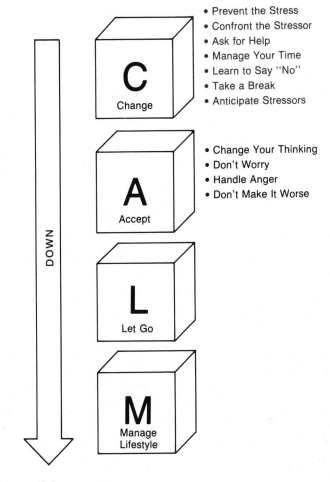

- Prevent the Stress
- Confront the Stressor
- Ask for Help
- Manage Your Time
- Learn to Say "No"
- Take a Break
- Anticipate Stressors

- Change Your Thinking
- Don't Worry
- Handle Anger
- Don't Make It Worse

C
Change

A
Accept

L
Let Go

M
Manage
Lifestyle

DOWN

FIGURE 3.1

requires maturity. Most of us find it easier to gripe and moan about a situation than to face it squarely and accept it for what it is.

If you have a completely unreasonable boss, and all efforts to improve communication or remove yourself from the situation have been unsuccessful, you are faced with how to manage the stress. You could participate with colleagues in telling "ain't it awful" stories, or you could complain to family and friends. These coping behaviors momentarily let off steam, but you remain upset about the situation. Following our model, the best way to manage this situation is to accept that you are working for a difficult boss, and there will be tensions between the two of you. Paradoxically, such acceptance is powerful; you gain a sense of control when you see things as they are. Wishing and complaining simply don't change reality and only deepen the stress you feel.

This is not to say you can't express dissatisfaction or disappointment with a situation. You can, and that can be healthy. Once it is expressed, however, move on. Expressing it over and over becomes complaining. Remember Fred who was planning the Annual Meeting in Chapter 2? He wanted an overhead projector for the meeting. When one wasn't available, he had several choices. He could complain to everyone he met that the meeting facility didn't follow through and that now the meeting wouldn't be as effective as he'd planned, or he could accept the reality of the situation and decide how he was going to cope with it. The second choice would reduce Fred's stress and the stress of those around him. He serves as an example to show others that they can move past disappointment.

CHANGE YOUR THINKING

You will find acceptance much easier if you are willing to change your perceptions and attitudes about the situation. Many times we create more stress internally with our thoughts than is ever caused by external events. As Epictetus said in the first century A.D., "Men are disturbed not by things, but by the views which they take of them."

If Fred says to himself, "This is awful! This could cost me my job! The President will be furious when he finds out there isn't an overhead projector. I knew I should have brought the projector myself!" he creates self-imposed stress. His thoughts give him more of a problem than the missing projector!

Dr. Albert Ellis, author of *A New Guide to Rational Living,* has developed an A-B-C model for understanding how our thoughts about a situation create our feelings and behavior. In his model, situations are neutral—neither positive nor negative. However, we form beliefs about situations, and these beliefs create feelings that lead to behaviors. Fred's beliefs and negative thoughts are going to cause him to feel frustrated, angry, and upset. That will result in some form of external behavior such as yelling at others, muscle tension, or self-criticism.

Imagine how differently Fred might behave if he thought, "Mistakes happen. This is certainly not the end of the world. I will alert the President and together perhaps we can come up with an alternative." With this kind of self-talk, Fred will feel in control, confident, and relaxed. He will approach the President in this frame of mind and be more likely to reach a satisfactory outcome.

Aside from the stress caused by physical stressors in the environment (for example, noise, air pollution, and furniture), all other stress is a result of perception or thoughts. To be able to accept reality for what it is without distorting it by criticizing, judging, or having other negative thoughts is a very powerful stress management technique.

You can check your thoughts against the following list of negative thoughts. The more of these you recognize in yourself, the greater the likelihood that you are creating stress for yourself. Put a check mark in front of any of the thought patterns you use.

_____ *Overgeneralization* There are two words that signal you are overgeneralizing: "always" and "never." These words distort reality, because situations neither "always" occur nor "never" occur. Both words lead to feelings of victimization, the opposite of the in-control feeling we need to manage stress. Let's look at an example.

Betsy is preparing to leave for a long-awaited 2-week vacation. At about 2:00 P.M., her boss comes in with an "urgent project—it has to be done before you leave." Betsy grudgingly takes the project, and as she starts to look through it thinks to herself, "I always get these last minute projects dumped on me. They never let you leave this place without trying to get one more thing out of you!"

How do you imagine Betsy is feeling? And how is she likely to interact with her boss the rest of the afternoon? Just by her thoughts she has created stress and will probably respond irritably to her boss and colleagues the rest of the afternoon. In addition, having activated the stress response, she is likely to have more difficulty concentrating on the task, which will further add to her stress.

To interrupt this negative pattern, Betsy needs to change her thinking. She would not compound her stress if she thought something like, "I will look at this and do the best I can in the time I have left."

_____ *All-or-Nothing Thinking*   In this form of negative thinking, you see things as extremes— either perfect and wonderful or imperfect and awful. There are no shades of gray. This, of course, is not the way reality is. To make a mistake is not the same thing as being a failure. To experience a disappointment is not the same thing as being unsuccessful. Not finishing a project is not the same as not starting it. To be less than "perfect" does not warrant criticism. See if you can identify the all-ornothing thinking in the situation below.

John did not receive the promotion he had applied for. This was the second time he had been passed over. While having lunch with one of his friends that day, he said, "Well, Steve, I've just about decided to change professions. It's pretty obvious that I'm not cut out to be an engineer. After all, I've been passed over twice now. I'll never get anywhere as an engineer. I'm just no good at it."

Because John is passed over for a promotion does not mean he is "not cut out to be an engineer," nor does it mean he will "never get anywhere." Did you catch the overgeneralization in that last phrase? John is adding to his disappointment by criticizing himself needlessly and viewing a disappointment as an indication that he cannot be successful.

He would lessen his stress while still acknowledging the disappointment if he said something different to himself and his friend. A more CALMing response might be, "I feel disappointed about not getting the promotion. This is the second time I've been passed over. I need to find out if I am missing a necessary skill, if my interview skills are weak, if

I lack some experience, or just where the problem lies. I still want that kind of position, and I'm willing to learn what I need to do to get that job in the future.''

Both this example and the previous one have something in common. With more positive responses, people stay focused on the present. They are not looking back with recriminations, and they are not looking forward with ''what ifs.'' To learn to stay in the here and now, or present to the moment, is a great stress reducer. The past and the future exist only in the mind. The present is current reality. Stress occurs when we leave present reality and worry about the past or future.

_____ *Mental Filter*   When you mental filter, your mind focuses on one aspect of a situation (usually negative) to the exclusion of anything else in the situation. It's almost as if that one part of the situation is magnetized, and it draws your undivided attention. Take the situation of Harriet, for example.

It was with excitement that Harriet opened the box with the new training catalog. This project had been nearly a year in the making. Then she saw it: The cover was not printed on the enamel paper stock she had ordered! As she flipped through the pages, she couldn't get her mind off of the cover. A colleague came over and picked up one of the catalogs. As he went through it he complimented Harriet on the design, layout, use of pictures, and detailed descriptions. For every positive remark he offered, Harriet countered with, ''Yeah, but did you see how dull the cover is?'' Harriet's mental filtering has not allowed her to notice any of the positive parts of her project. Even if someone else mentions them, she returns her focus to the one thing that is wrong. She's magnetized to what's wrong instead of what's right. Reality is that things go wrong and don't meet our expectations. To be unwilling to accept this is to mentally create stress for yourself. Harriet has lost her perspective by focusing on only one aspect of the situation. Through her mental filter all she can see is the wrong cover stock.

Harriet would be more effective if she handled the situation differently. Instead of focusing only on what she didn't like, Harriet could identify all the parts that pleased her as well as the parts that didn't. This is a more realistic assessment. Then, Harriet can decide if she wants to take any action to solve the problem of the covers. The covers may be less significant when Harriet is able to see the total picture. As long as she is using a mental filter, she is locked into the powerless position of being unable to take any action to change things. As soon as she changes her thinking she can move into a problem-solving mode.

_____ *Should, Ought, Must, Have To* Most people use these words as a regular part of their vocabularies. That is unfortunate, because these few words are responsible for many negative feelings and much low self-esteem. Each of these words represents not what we want to do or what we need to do, but what *someone else* thinks we need to do. They are relics of our past conditioning. Most "shoulds, oughts, musts, and have tos" come from our early childhood years. They may reflect wishes of our parents, our teachers, our Sunday school teachers, or any other authority figures. When we are young, we do not have the capability as adults do of reasoning. We do not discriminate about the information we take in, we just absorb it all. Then in adult life we find that some of those things work for us, and others do not. We have not learned, however, to "throw away" the messages that do not apply to us. Instead we carry them around in the form of "shoulds." When we encounter situations that trigger one of those childhood messages, we apply "should" to ourselves and feel guilty and often stressed. In the example below you will see how Tony uses this form of negative thinking to create stress for himself. He, too, was passed over for a promotion.

"I knew I should have worn the other suit. I just don't think they took me seriously enough. And when they asked me that question about my relationship with my boss, I never should have said there are times we disagree. I ought to know they don't want any troublemakers, and they probably thought I would be one from my answer. Why do I always have to say the wrong things in interviews? After as many interviews as I've had, I should handle them better by now."

How would *you* be feeling if you had just said this to yourself? Pretty inadequate, don't you think? Tony holds an underlying belief that he "should" be perfect. When reality shows he is not, he berates himself with "shoulds." In this way "shoulds" can be damaging to your self-esteem.

We also liberally apply "shoulds" to other people and their behavior. Whenever we do this, we are being judgmental, and the other people feel it. This is why you sometimes get a defensive reaction from another for no apparent reason. You probably have told them something they "should" or "shouldn't" do! As you go through this book, you will discover that, aside from this section and some examples, there are no shoulds, oughts, musts, or have tos. Most self-help books are filled with these judgmental phrases. By the time you reach the end, you feel guilty about all the things you aren't doing right or aren't doing at all.

In contrast, throughout this book you will be asked to "consider" ideas. At times you will be told gently of an action or behavior you "need" in order to reach your goals. At other times you will be advised on actions you will "want" to try for desired outcomes. These are the magic words—choose, consider, need, want—that you can start using to replace your shoulds, oughts, musts, and have tos. You will be astounded at the difference it makes in how you feel about yourself, and you will be equally impressed with the different response you get from others.

Let's go back to Tony and see how he could change his self-talk.

"At the next interview I need to wear a different suit. I believe I lost some of my credibility when I chose this one. I also want to handle the interview questions differently. It is probably wise to consider in advance how I will respond to the questions about my relationship with my boss. This time I wasn't prepared for the question and I did not come across the way I wanted to."

Now, wouldn't you feel differently about yourself after this kind of talk than after the other? If this was the only change you decided to make after reading this book, it would be a dramatic one!

_____ ***Disqualifying the Positive*** In this form of negative thinking you refuse to accept any positive feedback about yourself or your performance. If you receive a compliment, you find some way to turn it back to the sender or reduce its impact. It's a subtle form of discounting yourself and also, surprisingly enough, the person who gives you the positive feedback. Used on a regular basis, it is powerful enough to actually train others to not give you any compliments.

Watch how Molly responds in the next example when a colleague tells her what a great job she did getting the figures prepared for a marketing analysis.

"Oh, it was nothing, really. I just looked through some old reports and summarized their findings. Anybody could have done it if they took the time."

Can you see how Molly has discounted the feedback she received? Inadvertently she is telling her colleague, "What makes you think this was such a big deal? Aren't you exaggerating just a little?" Molly's reponse will put her colleague in the awkward position of trying to "convince" Molly to accept the compliment; or, she can withdraw the compliment. Either way, if this happens too many times, the colleague will decide it isn't worth the effort to give Molly any praise.

Molly could handle this situation better simply by saying, "Thank you." If she chose to, she could elaborate further and add, "It did take several hours to put together and I appreciate your noticing." This is also an opportunity for Molly to seek further information about her performance. If she is told she did a "great job," she can ask a clarifying question such as "What specifically did you like about it?" This gives her more information on how she can replicate this desirable performance in the future. These reponses all build Molly's self-esteem rather than eroding it. And as we will see in Chapter 5, self-esteem is one of the keys for managing stress.

_____*Jumping to Conclusions* With this thought pattern you make up an outcome to a situation. It may have some basis in fact, but your conclusion is usually an assumption. Then, you behave as if the often-faulty assumption is the truth. Let's look at an example. Don recently opened a new branch office. The sales figures so far are lower than he projected. This is what goes through his mind as he reviews the first quarter's figures.

"These figures are way below projections. I made the wrong decision to open this office. People in Corporate are probably going to want my resignation. Now I know why the VP hasn't returned my phone calls . . . he probably doesn't want to talk to me until after I get my notice from Personnel."

Don may have made an unwise decision; we all do so from time to time. Corporate may, in fact, want to discuss this with him. However, he is creating stress for himself before the fact by jumping to the conclusion that he will be asked to submit his resignation and that this is the reason his phone calls have not been returned. If Don had been told when he opened the new branch that failure to meet projections would result in dismissal, that's one thing. We can't assume that, though, from our example. As for the phone calls not being returned, we all know that is a too-common occurrence in business.

Don would be wiser to face reality clearly—he hasn't met projections—and to design a strategy for how to respond to this. Perhaps he will want to be proactive and call a meeting himself with senior management to discuss the shortfall. Maybe he will design a new tactic for getting the business he needs for the coming quarter. Either of these strategies puts him back in charge of the situation rather than feeling helpless and at the mercy of someone else.

When we jump to conclusions, it can also affect our future interactions with people. Don might begin to distance himself from senior management in anticipation of termination. If anyone offers suggestions, he may respond defensively or not at all, being convinced it won't matter anyway. His thoughts and beliefs create his own reality and his own destiny. For better or worse, we get what we expect.

_____ *Fortune-Telling* This resembles jumping to conclusions. When you are fortune-telling, you look into a crystal ball and predict the future. We all enjoy doing this from time to time, and there isn't anything wrong with doing it as long as you don't take it one more step and act as if that prediction is a truth. Let's look at Don's situation again. However, let's go back a little further in time to when he is considering opening a branch office. He has collected all the data in support of the new office and is reviewing them in his office. As he goes through the figures he thinks to himself, "Nah, Corporate will never go for this idea. They want sure-fire projects. I can't see them being willing to take a risk on this project. The numbers do look good, but I'm not setting myself up to be embarrassed when they turn the idea down.'' Don never submits his idea. He and the company lose, because while he's sitting there fortune-telling management's negative response, a competitor opens an office in the same location Don would have proposed. How many wonderful opportunities have been lost by American businesses because a creative employee engaged in fortune-telling and never took the risk of presenting his or her ideas? How many times have you not applied for a promotion, expected the worst from a new boss, or refused to make a decision because of fortune-telling? Replace your crystal ball with reality, and not only will you be more effective, you won't suffer from *imaginary* stress.

_____ **Labelling** Do you remember being taught as a child that "if you can't say something nice, don't say anything at all"? We need to recall that phrase when we are working with someone who doesn't meet our expectations or standards. We also need to be gentler with ourselves, particularly when we make errors. It is not necessary to attack and criticize ourselves or call ourselves names. That behavior only makes us feel bad inside, upsets us, and leads to increased stress. Even if you don't use labelling yourself, you've likely heard many of the following expressions used by others around the office:

"What a jerk!"

"I can't believe I'm so dumb."

"You can't talk sense to a crazy man."

"Only an idiot could do what I just did!"

And other, more colorful expressions!

Each of these statements leads to emotional upset. We certainly don't want to believe we can be like that. It is also extremely stressful to work with, for, or around someone who is like that. Also, these labels, like the other negative thoughts, distort reality. People cannot be described with a single label, positive or negative. We all change depending on the situations in which we find ourselves. Remember, from another person's point of view, his or her behavior makes perfect sense. You will reduce your stress by seeking to understand that point of view and reaching for a viewing point instead of using labels and thereby being judgmental.

As long as you judge others, you will judge yourself. Judgement is a source of stress and causes low self-esteem.

_____ **Catastrophizing** If you "make a mountain out of a molehill," you are catastrophizing. Put another way, it is like taking a snapshot of a problem, then having it blown up into a wall-size poster. In the process, the picture becomes distorted and you don't see the situation as it really is. Don was catastrophizing as well as jumping to conclusions in our earlier example. Not meeting projections for one quarter is hardly enough information on which to base a "go or no-go" decision. Often catastrophizing is accompanied by what ifs, each worse than the one preceding it, so that in just a few minutes you have gone from point A to point Z. Watch how this happens in the following example. Jean has just been told that one of her key staff members has resigned to take a position with a competitor. That afternoon Jean schedules an appointment with her boss to discuss the resignation. This is what she says.

"This is terrible! I don't know how we will get by without Debbie. She has more experience around here than anyone else. And where will I ever find someone with her skills and her ability to get along with others? You know she was the buffer in our department between Marsha and Doug. Now they will be fighting again. Plus, Debbie knew all our pricing strategies, which the competition will now have. She had such good relationships with her customers that they'll probably all move to the new company with her. You'd better prepare yourself for a bad quarter, this is going to be devastating!"

Does this sound exaggerated? Debbie may be a big loss to the company, but Jean has lost touch with reality and crossed over to catastrophizing. In the process, she is upsetting herself and failing to do what she needs, which is to begin to plan for how she will replace Debbie and to cover her assignments in the interim. Jean's thinking, not the situation, is the cause of this unnecessary stress. So far, she hasn't used any of her energy to reduce her stress or solve the problems she faces.

A better response when she meets with her boss might be, "Debbie has been a key employee here for years. She resigned today and that will have an impact on our customers and our department. Because she is going to a competitor, I think it is important that we quickly hire a replacement who can initiate contact with her customers. If we don't act soon, I 'm concerned some of them may follow her to her new employer. Will you authorize Personnel to begin an immediate search?''

There's quite a difference between the two ways of responding to the situation, isn't there? Are you beginning to see that no matter how difficult or challenging reality might be, it is consistently easier to respond to *it* than to the situations we create with our thoughts? The second step of the CALM method is to face reality and accept it. We don't need to embellish it. To do so will only create stress. You will discover that as you accept situations for what they are, you will also accept yourself.

Look back over the list of negative thoughts. How many check marks do you have? Are you willing to change any of these patterns? This is a good time to make a commitment to yourself to start accepting what you cannot change instead of making it worse with your thoughts.

DON'T WORRY

Sometimes we leave the present and drift into another time zone. We float into the past, where we re-hash what we did, what we decided, and what we said. We also may drift into the future and agonize about what might happen and what might not happen—what ifs. Neither of these behaviors is productive. Each is a form of worry that produces self-imposed stress.

Yet nearly all of us worry from time to time. What can you do if you're a worrier? There are several techniques you can use.

The first is to bring your worry into alignment with reality. Eighty percent of what we worry about never happens. Ten percent of what we worry about is going to happen, and there is not a thing we can do about it besides cope when it does. The last ten percent is made up of things whose impact we can reduce by taking action.

Take a moment right now and write down some of your worries. The list is already started for you with common worries identified by other business people.

1. What will happen to the economy?

2. Will I get the raise I want?

3. What does the boss think of me?

4. Do my colleagues like me?

5. Can I "get ahead?"

6. _____

7. _____

8. _____

Now, looking at your list of worries, ask yourself the following questions.

What is the worst that could happen? Think about what it is that you fear. Don't catastrophize, but look honestly at reality and identify the worst possible outcomes. Imagine that you are worried about which candidate to hire for a new staff position. What is the worst that could happen? You might make the wrong decision and need to go through the same process again in a few months. Give yourself enough time to think through all your fears.

How likely is it that the worst will happen? Keeping your worst fear in mind, assign a percentage to the probability it will occur. If you think it's not very likely, ask yourself what that means: 20 percent, 10 percent, 5 percent? Be as specific as you can. Our manager might decide there is a 4 percent chance this candidate won't work out and he will need to start the process over. Already we are beginning to put this concern into perspective. Once you do this, you can leave the worry behind.

Could you live with it if the worst happened? Notice we are not asking if you would like it or be happy with it, we're asking if you could live with it. If your worst-case scenario did happen, it undoubtedly would be difficult to cope with, but could you live with it? Our manager, if honest, will say yes, he could live with it. Firing the first candidate, beginning the search process anew, and then training another person may not be how he would like to spend his time and energy; however, he could do it. With this question, you are testing your personal strengths and resources. You're asking yourself if you could come to accept this worst situation. It is extremely rare for people to answer "no" to this question when they force themselves to be totally honest.

If the worst does happen, how will you cope? This question helps you project yourself into the future. This is the planning, or rehearsal, stage. What would you do? As you are able to picture yourself handling the situation, you build confidence and regain control. Difficult though it might be, you already can visualize what you might do. Our manager knows exactly what the qualifications are for the job; he would pull out the old advertisements and reuse them in the paper. Before he placed an ad, though, he would recontact his second choice candidate and see if she is still available. He might not even need to advertise again!

This step actually allows you to be more proactive today. By anticipating the worst and beginning to plan for it, you can build into your activities right now things that will make coping with your worst-case scenario easier if you ever are faced with it.

After this mental exercise, many people find their worries shrink to a manageable size. They regain control instead of feeling at the mercy of the obsessive worry.

Will the intellectual analysis work in all cases? No, sometimes you need another technique called "thought stopping." This technique works just the way it sounds—you stop the obsessive worry thought. You do this by noticing your thought process. You become an observer of your own mind. And as soon as you start to worry, tell yourself, "Stop!" Your purpose is to interrupt the worry thought.

Picture the child's game of musical chairs. The music is playing and the children are walking in a circle around a row of chairs. Suddenly the music stops, and one of the chairs is pulled away. Someone is out of the game. Worry sends you running around in circles like the music does. When you stop the thought—that is, turn off the music—you can pull the chair out from under worry. The game is over. Once you interrupt the worry thought, you will need to replace it with something else; another thought that is positive and soothing. Try replacing worry with its opposite. If you're worried about choosing the wrong job applicant, replace that thought with, "I make wise decisions." Such positive thoughts are called *affirmations.* We will talk about them in more depth in Chapter 4. It is even more helpful if you take a deep, slow breath as you say the affirmation to yourself. The deep breath helps you relax.

This technique takes some practice, and you may need to use it many times in the course of a day for a particularly dominant worry thought. However, if each time you worry you use this technique, gradually it will recede into the background and you'll need to use the technique less often.

Some people have found the "Scarlett O'Hara technique" to be a great aid in overcoming these obsessive thoughts. (Scarlett O'Hara was the heroine in *Gone with the Wind* who handled her problems by saying to herself, "I'll think about that tomorrow.") To try this for yourself you will need a small notebook or pad of paper (and pen or pencil) that you can keep with you at all times. If at any time throughout the day you catch yourself starting to worry about something, pull out your pad and jot it down. As you write, say to yourself as Scarlett O'Hara did, "I'll think about that tomorrow." To be fair with yourself, designate a period each day, perhaps 15 to 30 minutes, to review your worry list and give it your undivided attention. Concentrated worry is more productive than worry that is slipped in among your normal daily activities. As you become better at this, you will notice you are able to complete your worry in less and less time, until one day you'll notice you don't seem to be spending any time on worry!

The last strategy you can use to reduce worry is helpful for those ten percent of the cases in which what you're worried about probably will happen and you can do something about it. In these cases, you need to go beyond the circular, nonproductive worry process and move yourself to take action. Whether your action is successful or not is less important than your doing something. As soon as you begin to act, you regain some control over your life. In that respect, worry and procrastination are very similar. The only way out of procrastination is to get started on the task, no matter how small or insignificant the start. The act of starting breaks its strangle hold. So it is with worry. To initiate some action, no matter how small, will help you reduce stress and restore your personal power. Our manager who is struggling with which candidate to choose might check references rather than agonize over whether he was making the right decision or not. If the situation turns out to be your worst-case scenario, do something to reduce your fear or something to strengthen your ability to cope.

Each of these strategies can help you overcome worry, although each takes time and effort. Remember that to take no action will leave you in the same place 6 months or 6 years from now. If you begin today to change some of the things that are causing you stress, your life can be very different in just a few short months.

If all else fails, get yourself a copy of the 1988 hit record, "Don't Worry . . . Be Happy" by Bobby McFerrin.

HANDLE YOUR ANGER

It is a normal response to be disappointed when things do not happen the way we want them to. Thus, if we are faced with a situation we cannot change, disappointment can be expected. Often anger will accompany disappointment, although it is not usually helpful.

If you travel by plane you probably have seen examples of nonproductive anger. Jack was in the Memphis airport waiting for a connection that was delayed owing to bad weather. He had already been there 4 hours when he heard some yelling and a string of obscenities. He turned to see another passenger, red in the face and fists clenched, screaming at the ticket agent about the delay. The ticket agent was trying to be as calm and polite as possible in that situation, but it was easy to see he, too, was upset. Jack just chuckled to himself, "Didn't that guy realize all the yelling in the world would not change the weather?" A little while later Jack approached the ticket counter and expressed his concern over the behavior of the other passenger. The ticket agent smiled and said, "Well, I decide who gets first option on the few available seats on the next flight." Then Jack calmly requested a meal voucher, since he had now been in the airport 5 hours, and the ticket agent pleasantly complied.

In this situation, how could anger help? It couldn't. The upset passenger raised his blood pressure, embarrassed himself in front of others, and lessened his chances of getting what he wanted—a flight out of Memphis. Of course he wanted to be on his way; so did all the other passengers. Once he realized he could not change the situation, though, anything he did to delay accepting reality only increased his stress.

Recall a time when you were angry. Did the anger help you? Did it reduce the stress you felt at the time, or did it worsen the level of stress you were experiencing? If you are honest with yourself, you probably will say the anger did not help the situation.

Anger is what is known as a "secondary emotion." That means it comes second, after another feeling—usually hurt, fear, or powerlessness. It tends to mask these feelings which make us more vulnerable, from ourselves, and others. To be able to accept the things we cannot change means we will need to come to terms with these underlying feelings. When they are protected by anger, it takes longer. First the anger needs to be resolved, then you can resolve the underlying feelings, and finally you can reach acceptance.

Ironically, anger does not protect us quite as well as we have thought. Research studies have monitored the effect of anger on the body. Rather than protecting us, it actually weakens the immune system. "Scientists who have studied responses to stress have found that ineffectual anger is the emotion most destructive to homeostasis. A serene acceptance of *what is* promotes health, but by keeping the mind clear it also puts a person in a better position to change things that need changing.''[1]

Think about a person or a situation that has made you angry. As you bring that image vividly into your mind, notice how you feel. Are your muscles getting tense? Can you feel your jaw starting to tighten? Is your heart racing? How do you feel emotionally? Are you aware of becoming upset or anxious inside? These are the common responses to anger.

If we use these feelings as a signal that we need to take action, anger can be productive. When you notice yourself feeling anger, you want to accept it for what it is, express it or let go of it, and gently move on. Too often we notice feelings of anger, but take no action. Instead we replay what we are angry about over and over, keeping ourselves perpetually upset and stressed.

Acceptance paves the way for new action and facilitates managing the stressor. When Jack accepted that his flight was going to be delayed several hours, he freed himself to act. Did he want to read a book, do some paperwork, make phone calls, or talk with other passengers? He was free to move on and go ahead with his life. His angry fellow passenger lost all those hours in emotion. He was not able to choose to act, and his energy was consumed by *reaction.*

If you are aware of feeling anger, what specifically can you do to get rid of it? There are several things you can do. You can start by looking underneath it for the primary feeling. What is scaring or threatening you? Who or what hurt you? Do you feel helpless or powerless? This may not be easy to identify at first, because we want to protect ourselves from this pain. However, if you continue to mull over these questions, the answer will become apparent. Often this will dissolve the anger, because you see what you were trying to protect. If the anger is directed toward another person, you may want to express it. A four-step model which works very well follows.

Step One. Express how you are feeling. Own up to the angry or upset feelings. To do this, you will use an "I" statement, which we discussed in Chapter 2. You could start with the simple phrase, "I feel angry. . . ."

Step Two. Explain briefly what situation is upsetting you. Be as objective as you can. This is not the time to blame or attack someone, nor is it the time for a 30-minute discussion of the situation. Keep it short, simple, and direct.

Step Three. This is the tough part. Now you are going to expose the underlying feeling that is causing the anger. With this step, you take the risk of letting the other person know how you really are feeling. Remember, anger is a secondary emotion that is protecting you from your vulnerable feelings of hurt, fear, or powerlessness. This step is the most powerful of this four-step process. Most of us drop our defensiveness and hostility toward others when they show their true feelings. As you become more practiced with this step, you will discover you feel anger less often. This is because you will learn to notice the primary feelings earlier and express them directly without masking them with anger.

Step Four. This is an optional step in which you may ask for a specific remedy to your hurt or fear.

This is especially appropriate when the anger is a result of a misunderstanding. This step can create some new avenues for communicating that might prevent the situation from recurring.

Let's look at an example of this process in action. Glenn's company has redesigned its offices, and now instead of a private office, he has a cubicle. Glenn is mad about this change and tells anyone who will listen to him. It has been 3 weeks now, and although other people seem to be adapting to the change, he is still mad. He finally realizes that others are beginning to tire of his constant complaining, so he decides to try this process. The most difficult part is Step 3, in which he tries to figure out why he is so mad. Of what could he be afraid? Nothing comes to mind. What or who has hurt him? As he ponders this question, it comes to him. He feels hurt that his work as a personnel specialist has not been considered worthy of a private office. Glenn feels the information about salary and benefits he is providing to job applicants is confidential. He doesn't feel comfortable talking about these issues when he knows someone in the next cubicle can overhear him. With this awareness, he schedules an appointment with his boss to discuss the problem.

"Peter, I feel upset about losing my enclosed office for a cubicle. Much of the work I do is confidential, and I feel discounted by not having an appropriate workspace. I need your help in coming up with a way to do my job and still ensure the confidentiality of each interview."

In this example, Glenn has accepted his cubicle as his office and is able to go beyond it to take action to get his needs met. There are any number of solutions he and his boss may try—from getting a machine that produces white noise for confidentiality, to giving Glenn access to a private office or conference room where he can meet with candidates. Like other emotions, once anger is identified and expressed, it tends to disappear. Don't let anger prevent you from accepting the things you cannot change.

DON'T MAKE IT WORSE

When we don't like situations, we sometimes engage in a variety of counterproductive behaviors to avoid accepting reality. We just discussed anger, which is one such behavior, but there are others. These are all "copers," quick fixes that give short-term relief with long-term price tags.

Resentment

When we refuse to express our anger or let go of it, we build up resentments and hold grudges. We actually give our power to other people because we stay upset about something they did or said. The other people are not suffering! They may not even know we are upset. This passive emotion suppresses the immune system.

Complaining

It is not pleasant to listen to a constant complainer. Don't let yourself fall into this category. Complaining is a passive reaction that does not give you any control. It is a reactive response that results in feelings of helplessness. The mindset is one of wishful thinking. That is, if you complain long enough or to the right people, something will be done. Complaining will not change bad weather, nor will it change modular furniture into private offices. It keeps your emotions stirred up, with no chance of resolution. Replace complaining with acceptance of the situation and a plan of action.

Revenge

You no doubt have heard the expression, "Don't get mad, get even." Neither getting mad nor getting even will resolve stress. Plotting revenge against a person or a company keeps you embroiled emotionally, without any release from the stress. Revenge does not solve problems; it is an indirect means of addressing conflict. Be mature enough to express yourself and get on with your life. There is another axiom that is true: "What goes around, comes around." Your negative behavior will come back to haunt you. Remember that if the other party has been in the wrong, he or she also is subject to this universal principle.

Attacking

Company gossip can fall anywhere on a wide continuum, from interesting and relatively harmless to malicious. Don't allow yourself to attack other people behind their backs. If you are upset, use one of the skills we have outlined for expressing anger or handling conflict. Like the other negative coping strategies we've discussed, this does not remove the stress, but keeps it churning inside you. Focus on ways to disagree with a person's ideas without attacking the person. Confront the individual rather than feeding the rumor mill.

Work Slowdowns

Some workers, when they feel stress due to an interpersonal conflict or an unpopular decision, make a deliberate effort to lower their productivity. This is much like revenge and similarly will come back to haunt you. When you know you are giving less than your best effort, you lower your self-esteem. This behavior does nothing to change the stressor. As a coping mechanism, such an action has a short-term benefit before the long-term costs start accumulating.

Self Pity

Feeling sorry for yourself will not change the situation, nor will it make you feel any better. When you feel self-pity, you give away your power and assume a helpless role in the situation. It is perfectly okay to feel bad or disappointed when things do not go your way; to continue feeling bad isolates you and adds to the stress you were already feeling.

SUMMARY

In summary, there are some things you cannot change. You need to let go of the desire to control them or make them the way you want them. This gentle act is empowering, in that as you choose to let go of control, you gain control. This paradoxical process brings long-term release from stress. Reactive strategies may *feel* like a release from stress, but in the long-term they lead to increased stress. These short-term strategies include negative thoughts, worry, anger, resentment, complaining, revenge, attacking, self-pity, and work slowdowns.

REFERENCE

1. Bernie S. Siegel, *Love, Medicine and Miracles.* (New York, New York: Harper and Row Publishers, 1986), 192.

4

The *L* of CALM: *Let Go*

Most of us know more about "holding on" and "adding on" than we know about "letting go." This causes us a great deal of stress. In this chapter, we want to explore how you can begin the gentle process of letting go of your attachments to negative beliefs, unrealistic expectations, dysfunctional relationships, and unreasonable commitments. When you do, you'll free yourself for more creativity and enjoyment in your life.

HOLDING ON

This occurs when you attempt to maintain everything in your life exactly as it is, even though it may no longer be useful or productive. This is seen often when a peer is promoted to manager. The new

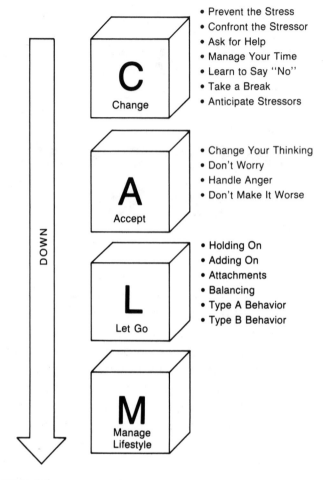

Figure 4.1

manager moves into a new role and still holds on to former responsibilities. Rather than training someone to take over the previous job, he or she holds on to control. Take the case of Jeff, who started with a small manufacturing firm at an entry-level position. Over the years, he moved up the ranks until he became Manager of Manufacturing. He was responsible for revenues of over $60 million, and yet people within the company could not change offices without his approval! He was still making decisions that would have been better made by lower levels of management. This also occurs with entrepreneurial ventures. In the early days, the entrepreneur or founder needs to do everything, but as the company grows, she needs to let go and assign these tasks to others. Some insist on holding on, to their personal and corporate detriment.

Sadly, many people choose to hold on to past disappointments, frustrations, or disagreements with others. This keeps them locked in the past instead of in the present. As we discussed in Chapter 2, whenever we lose sight of the present reality by thinking about either the past or the future, we are inviting stress. This type of holding on creates stress for others because of the tension that surrounds keeping grudges, disappointments, or frustrations alive.

Pat, who worked in a financial institution, held on to every negative experience she had, not only in her professional life, but also in her personal life. In the cafeteria, she was the first to recount how she was mistreated, passed over, or misunderstood. Just the mention of certain people's names was enough to send her off on a tirade. Pat never seemed to have a good day or be happy. Colleagues knew that crossing her was the same as initiating a cold war. She suffered from ulcers and felt perpetually upset, uptight, and angry. Too bad she couldn't let go of some of those petty grievances and release herself from the upset she was feeling.

Feelings

Each of us experiences a range of feelings during the day. To some of these we assign positive labels, and to others we assign negative labels. Thus, we arbitrarily decide that one feeling is more desirable than another. The reality, of course, is that a feeling is a feeling, nothing more or less. A wide range of feelings makes up the human experience. Just as there can be no darkness without light, there can be no joy without sadness.

It is not, therefore, feelings that create problems or stress for us. Rather, it is the meanings we assign to feelings and how attached we become to those meanings.

Craig learned this through some painful experiences. While at a departmental meeting, he became angry with his Vice President. The two of them exchanged harsh words, and afterwards Craig felt bad. On another day, he got into a dispute with a client about a bill. The client protested the bill was wrong and became loud and rude. Craig left the encounter feeling hurt and angry himself. On another occasion, someone from the office "borrowed" one of his files and did not return it. Craig spent over an hour tracking it down. He felt disgusted that someone would take something without asking. After a period of time, he found himself increasingly upset and distressed about such incidents, until he became depressed and disillusioned with people in general.

He was describing this to a friend when the friend said, "You know, Craig, it's as if you're constantly dragging around a big bag of bones. Every time something happens that disappoints you, doesn't meet your expectations, or hurts you, you pick it up like a bone and throw it in the bag. After all these years you're carrying an awfully heavy bag. In fact, I can see it is literally weighing you down. If I were you, I'd do two things. First, I would stop collecting bones! Second, I would look in that bag and pull out a few bones at a time, give them one last look over, and throw them away! No one is suffering except you. Most of those hurts you carry around are known only to yourself.''

Craig gave these comments considerable thought and decided his friend was right. He made a promise to himself not to add any more bones to his bag and to systematically throw out all the bones he had been carrying.

How many bad feelings do you carry around? To let go of them means you will need to forgive others. Don't get mad, and don't get even—release the feelings, let go of them. Holding on and carrying them with you can only make you feel bad and will do nothing to change the situation. A colleague just may have been informed that an account was lost when you walk in to make a request. The boss snaps at you, and you leave feeling hurt and angry. Stop. Let go of the hurt and anger and forgive that person for being short-tempered. You will feel better and have more to offer the next person you meet. If you hold the anger, you will rehearse the scene over and over in your mind in instant replays of your unpleasant feelings that churn you up inside. You are living in the past, not the present.

Forgiveness, like acceptance (Chapter 3), is deceptive; it is an active process that puts you in control.

You may be surprised to discover how many bad feelings you hold on to. Forgiveness lightens your load, reduces your stress, and reduces the stress of others around you. Remember that this is Step 3 of the CALM model. In Step 1 you change the things you can, which might mean asserting your rights with another person. It might mean confronting someone about how his or her behavior is affecting you. At Step 1, you may get a change in behavior that solves the problem. You would not need to progress through the model. If there is no change after you confront someone, you may need to accept the situation for what it is. Then, in Step 3, instead of holding on to negative feelings about the situation, let go of them and forgive the other person.

Beliefs

In Chapter 3 we discussed the A-B-C model of how beliefs can cause feelings. Unfortunately, many of us are holding on to beliefs that do not serve us well. In some cases, what we believe comes from childhood programming and may not even be true! Our belief systems, when they are not consistent with reality, can be a source of stress for us if we become attached to them. Let's look at an example.

Hiro was feeling anxious and upset. He had spent years working with audiovisual equipment, including video equipment. His company had secured some film taken by a local television station of one of their plants in operation. Hiro was going to edit it to create an employee-training film. After noting what excerpts he wanted to use, he set up the dubbing equipment. When he finished transferring the film he rewound it and discovered he had pressed "record" instead of "play." Not only did he not have the excerpts for his training film, he had erased the original! For a week Hiro nearly made himself sick with worry, wondering how he could ever tell his boss. He couldn't believe he could make such a dumb mistake. He was an expert with video equipment; how could he have pushed the wrong button?

We all make mistakes. None of us is perfect. Hiro had a belief that because he was trained and experienced, he could not make a mistake. In his mind, there was no excuse or explanation for his error. It was this belief that was upsetting him more than the lost tape. To expect yourself to be perfect is what Dr. Albert Ellis would call an irrational belief. When you notice yourself feeling disproportionately stressed or upset about a situation, you can bet there is an irrational belief operating.

You may recognize some of these more common beliefs that get us into trouble:

1. You must have love and approval from all people.

2. You must be totally competent, adequate, and achieving.

3. You have to view things as awful, horrible, or terrible when you are frustrated, treated unfairly, or rejected.

4. Unhappiness comes from factors outside your control, and you can't control them.

5. If something seems frightening or scary, you should dwell on it as if it will occur.

6. It is easier to avoid than to face life's difficulties.

7. Your past is all-important and should affect your present life.

This is only the beginning of a list of beliefs to which most of us can relate. Each of us carries internally a set of beliefs that creates stress for us. What are some of your beliefs?

As we become attached to these beliefs, we begin to expect the world to operate in compliance with them. If it does not, we experience stress. Let's look at another example.

Marta believed in the Golden Rule—"Do unto others as you would have others do unto you." Consequently, whenever she went out for lunch, she asked if anyone in the office would like her to bring something back for them. Over time she began to feel resentful; no one ever asked her if she wanted something when they went out. She expected them to behave as she did and check with her before they went to lunch. When they didn't, she felt used and angry.

Can you see how Marta used her beliefs to create expectations? She attached meaning to the fact that her expectations weren't met, saying something like, "Those people are inconsiderate," and she felt bad.

A better approach would be for Marta to use her assertive skills to take charge of her life by asking her colleagues directly for what she wants. In Chapter 3, we discussed several types of negative thinking that can create stress for us. Whenever you say the word "should," there is an underlying belief. As an experiment, notice your shoulds for the rest of the day, and see if you can identify the underlying beliefs. Then, ask yourself if those beliefs are based on reality. Here are a few examples to get you started:

Should I should have gotten the Carter account.

Belief I need to succeed at everything I do.

Should Dick should have turned in his monthly report when it was due.

Belief It's not okay for someone to disappoint me.

Should I should have called when I knew I was running late.

Belief It's not okay to make a mistake.

Now add your own to the list.

Should _____

Belief _____

What can you do when these dysfunctional beliefs begin to create unnecessary stress? Let go of them and begin to replace them with more realistic beliefs. Using the examples above, we can convert the beliefs into preferences instead of demands.

Belief I need to succeed at everything I do.

Revised I like to succeed; it feels good. Although I would like to succeed at everything I do, I realize and accept that this is not possible.

Belief It's not okay for someone to disappoint me.

Revised I would prefer not to be disappointed. However, the reality is that I will be disappointed from time to time. People will not always honor their promises and commitments. I can accept that others are not perfect.

Belief It's not okay to make a mistake.

Revised I prefer not to make mistakes, although I realize I will from time to time. Each mistake is an opportunity for me to learn and grow.

Now, see if you can revise your unreasonable beliefs into more rational preferences. Once you begin to see "preferences" or "wants" instead of demands, you dramatically reduce your internal stress.

Belief _____

Revised _____

Remember when you completed Braham's Work Stress Inventory (Chapter 1)? Although external events may be the source of some of the stress in your life, by far the greatest source of stress is your internal belief system and resultant self-talk. Some people who suffer physically from stress have practically no external stressors. Their symptoms come directly from their unreasonable expectations. External stressors are exponentially worsened when there are irrational beliefs operating.

Examine your beliefs, and change those that create stress for you.

Things

We also hold on to things, not unlike children. When parents try to teach a child to share, the child clutches each toy they propose to give away and refuses to let go of it. Some of us maintain this behavior long into adulthood. Sarah worked for such a man. Everything that came into the office was to be filed. Nothing could be thrown away. The file cabinets were bulging. It was increasingly difficult to find the important things because of all the unimportant ones Sarah needed to wade through. Sarah hated to go into his office; it was the home of a true "pack rat," as she called him. More time was wasted trying to find something on his desk than she cared to admit. She often thought of the joy she'd feel if she came in some Saturday, brought a two-ton dumpster, and started to pitch things into it!

If Sarah's boss could learn to let go of some of that paper and clutter, he would be more effective and reduce the stress of those around him.

People

Finally, we hold on to people. Mike was this way. He had a couple of guys in the department who weren't really doing their jobs. He had talked with them on several occasions, but nothing seemed to change. They weren't bad guys; in fact, they were the nicest employees you could find anywhere. They simply didn't have the skills they needed to do the job. Mike continued to keep them on the payroll, even though others in the department had to do extra work to carry the slack. This created low morale among the people who were always doing a little more than their share. However, Mike thought it wasn't too much to ask when these two guys were so nice and tried so hard.

Has Mike done anyone a favor? No. He is holding on to two nonproductive employees at their own expense, and at the expense of the rest of the department. There may be another place in the company where these people could contribute in a meaningful way. If Mike had a department filled with people who could do their jobs, he would increase morale and reduce everyone's stress. But he holds on under the misconception that he is being nice. Meanwhile, he, too, suffers under the pressure of a department that is perpetually behind in its work.

We begin to see that holding on is pervasive. We hold onto people, things, feelings, beliefs, and expectations. Some of us hold onto all these; others have a favorite one or two. What do you hold on to? How does that create stress for you?

ADDING ON

In addition to holding on, many of us "add on." When asked, we agree to take on new projects, join new committees, or cultivate new clients, in addition to our existing schedules. This works out for a while, but as a long-term strategy, it is fraught with stress. Any structure, no matter how strong, can take only so much pressure before it starts to weaken and eventually break. The human body is not exempt from this basic principle. Take Charlie's situation.

Charlie was a star in the company. Bright, likeable, and a quick thinker, he was sought out by many others. This flattered Charlie, and he usually agreed to help out. One day, though, he noticed heart palpitations and a tingling down his arm. When he went to see his family doctor, he was asked to describe his work. Charlie explained that he loved it. He was involved in a number of special projects throughout the company, sat in on most committee meetings, and managed another department while its manager was on short-term disability. Charlie was also on call for the training department people, who used him at least once a quarter for some of their technical training. The doctor looked Charlie directly in the eye after hearing all this and said, "Charlie, if you don't start prioritizing and letting go of some of those commitments, you won't be around for anybody much longer."

Charlie needs to go back to Step 1 of the CALM model and learn to say "no." We can change a potentially stressful situation by letting go instead of adding on.

ATTACHMENTS

The process of letting go is simple, yet difficult. It is paradoxical. Letting go is a decision you make, and then you allow it to happen. We hold on or add on out of fear. What will be left if we let go? Who will we be? What will others think? As Marilyn Ferguson says in *The Aquarian Conspiracy,* "It's not so much that we're afraid of change, or so in love with the old ways, but it's that place in between we fear . . . it's like being in between trapezes. It's Linus when his blanket is in the dryer. There's nothing to hold on to."

Our tendency to attach ourselves to beliefs, people, things, and expectations makes letting go so tough. As we discussed in Chapter 3, situations in and of themselves are neither positive nor negative; they exist. Period. We give each situation, each interaction with another human being, and each thought we think all their meaning. Such meaning comes from nowhere else. Why do we dread Mondays and celebrate Fridays? There is no reason, other than the meaning we choose to give each of those days. Why do we become upset with ourselves if we make mistakes? We do so because we have attached meaning to doing things right. Why do we stay upset for months after losing a promotion? We do it because we equate the promotion with self-esteem. Only one person gives these situations their meaning—you. In the following example, see how Connie created stress for herself because of her attachments to people.

The cake had been brought out, party horns were blowing, and everyone was celebrating. Everyone that is, except Connie. She felt like running away or crying. Two of her key employees were retiring. They had been with the company for over 25 years. What would she do? The department just couldn't run without them. They knew so much of the company's history and so many reasons why things were done as they were. They had given her so much support. Connie felt abandoned, deserted, and depressed.

Did Connie need to experience this much stress? No. It is sad to see longtime employees leave. Their friendship and their contributions to the department will be missed. However, is it the end of the department or of productive work relationships? No. Connie has attached herself to these people. By giving their leaving such significance, she upsets herself. If she can let go of them while remembering the good times and their contributions, she can move on without the overwhelming stress.

The second aspect to letting go of attachments is to face the reality that things change all the time. To hold on to what is, hoping to keep it the same, is to guarantee disappointment and stress. Each moment gives way to the next. In every ending there is a beginning. The ability to grow is directly proportionate to the ability to let go. The ability to stay calm and relaxed is directly proportionate to the ability to let go. Visualize yourself holding on to something, perhaps an umbrella in a strong wind. Can you feel the muscle tension as you try to resist the wind and its tug on your umbrella? Now, compare that feeling with one of letting go of the umbrella—releasing all that muscle tension and no longer resisting or fighting. That is the difference between holding on and letting go. We enact this drama with our bodies every day, often all day. We habitually hold our breath, rather than easily and naturally letting it out. When we do allow ourselves to let go, we experience the "sigh of relief."

If you are going to climb a ladder, there is only one way to get to the top. You will need to let go of the rung you are holding before you can reach for the next one. The principle is the same whether it's an aluminum ladder or a career ladder!

When you begin to let go of your attachments, you will make a discovery: You will feel a profound sense of freedom. There won't be so much "noise" in your mind. There will be space in your life for solitude. We need some moments of quiet for ourselves. We need time to think, time to create, and time to renew ourselves. Solitude can provide this.

How many of us have used the expression, "I can't hear myself think"? We can hear our thoughts only when we simplify our lives enough that we have time to listen. That's what letting go does. It starts to simplify things. You can see more clearly when the clutter is out of the way.

BALANCING

When we are holding on or adding on, our lives get out of balance. We add more work commitments and suddenly notice we have become estranged from our families. We hold on to old methods and procedures for doing things at the office and realize we're out of touch with the present. We haven't kept up with new technology, new processes, and new knowledge; consequently, we may be passed over for promotions.

Balance is a delicate and ongoing process. If you tip it, you will pay a price physically, emotionally, intellectually, or interpersonally. The body's natural state is to be in balance. When that is disrupted, the body will adapt naturally in an effort to restore itself. That adaptation, as we saw in Chapter 1, often comes in the form of symptoms. In fact, if you are experiencing symptoms, it is helpful to view them as the body's attempt to communicate with you—to tell you that you are no longer in balance. If you heed this message, you can take action to assist the body to regain its balance and thereby reduce your stress. The more you close your ears, either by refusing to pay attention to the message or by medicating it away so you can't hear it any longer, the more you force your body to escalate its adaptation efforts.

Through solitude, you can learn to create a place of quiet within you that you can access whenever you need it. You literally can let go of the pressures of the moment to retreat to your inner place, where you can think through what you need to do. Solitude helps us restore balance. It is the purposeful choice, rather than the body's imposition, of downtime. Chapter 5 describes some ways to create this solitude. Without this you will react and adjust to and cope with stress, rather than following the CALM model and managing the stress.

People who do not learn to let go and release themselves from stress can and do burn out. The ultimate outcome is that they are *forced* to let go. Sadly, they may let go of their jobs, their health, their relationships with others, and their self-esteem. When you reach the burnout stage, you do not choose what you will let go. It is out of your control. How much better it is to learn to let go along the way, to keep the choices within your power, and to prevent burnout. One way or the other, you will let go, and it is your choice to either control the process or let it control you.

With time, you come to know yourself better; you can differentiate between what you want and need and what someone else wants or expects you to do. You gain greater control over your own life through clarity about what you want. You can make choices about what's important more easily. At forty, many people are still trying to figure out what they want to be when they grow up. That's in part because they haven't had time with themselves to contemplate the question.

So, letting go has two levels of benefits. On one level we do not hold onto stressors or add new ones. This gives us some time for ourselves—an opportunity to experience some moments of solitude in which we can continue to clarify what is important in our lives, and where we want to invest our limited time and energies. The second benefit is that we are more able to stay in the present and experience a physical and emotional freedom that is not possible when we rigidly cling to people, things, beliefs, or expectations. The process enables us to restore balance to our lives, which is critical to health and well-being. To let go is the single best way to prevent burnout.

TYPE A BEHAVIOR

Dr. Meyer Friedman first identified what we now refer to as *Type A behavior*. It is a cluster of traits that in research studies has consistently made an individual more vulnerable to heart disease. According to Dr. Friedman's research, people with Type B behavior practically can be guaranteed they will not suffer a heart attack before age sixty or sixty-five. Type As can be given no such guarantee. In other words, if you or someone you know has had a heart attack before age sixty to sixty-five, you can be 99 percent sure their Type A behavior was a key cause.

To find out what your stress personality is, ask yourself these questions:

1. Do you try to be on time for all meetings and appointments?

2. Would you describe yourself as competitive?

3. Do you like to do several things at the same time, like talk on the phone and read your mail?

4. Do you feel rushed most of the time?

5. Do you do things fast, for instance, walk fast, talk fast, or eat fast?

6. Do you spend most of your time at work to the exclusion of other activities?

7. Do you feel upset if you have to wait, whether in line, for traffic, or for an appointment?

If you answered "yes" to four or more questions, you exhibit Type A behavior. Less than four "yes" answers describes Type B behavior.

The Type A personality is composed of a cluster of behaviors including competitiveness, hurry sickness, and aggressiveness or hostility. It is the last characteristic—hostility—that is most responsible for health-related problems. Just what causes it is not completely clear, although there does seem to be a connection between low self-esteem and the behavior.

Low Self-Esteem

How you *feel* about yourself is the way you measure self-esteem. The more you like and accept yourself, the higher your self-esteem. Sadly, many people do not like themselves very much. Consequently they engage in any number of behaviors to compensate for the low opinion they hold of themselves.

For example, some people go out of their way to "do good and be nice." The logic is that if they are good enough people they will like themselves and, in the interim at least, others also will like them. They are frequently taken advantage of, because it is difficult for them to say "no."

Some of us boast about our accomplishments, who we know, what we own or where we've been. We try to project an air of importance. We think that if others think we are important they will like us, and in the process we may come to like ourselves. However, we usually are perceived as arrogant or egotistical. Self-acceptance rarely results.

Others with low self-esteem try to hide from the world, and not be noticed. They experience feelings of worthlessness and do not feel they deserve to be included or treated with respect. They have trouble expressing how they feel or what they want. Some express their low self-esteem by putting themselves in situations in which they are mistreated, abused, or punished. They seem to want to show the world just how "bad" they really are. They expect to be treated like the "not-okay" people they believe themselves to be. These people are many of society's misfits and victims.

Still others seek to feel okay about themselves through accomplishment. In their minds, the more they are able to achieve the more worthy they are. If they can just achieve enough, they will be graced with the "I'm okay" feeling. This incessant drive to do more, achieve more, and accomplish more, underlies Type A behavior, and leads to stress.

However the low self-esteem is expressed, it hurts the person who doesn't like himself or herself. While we are most concerned in this book about the person who copes with low self-esteem through doing, achieving, and accomplishing, the following suggestions can help you feel better about yourself no matter how your low self-esteem manifests itself.

Affirmations We talked in Chapter 3 about negative self-talk and how it can create stress for you. If you decide to change that self-talk, you will need to replace it with something else, something more positive—affirmations.

An affirmation is a positive statement you say to yourself that affirms you. It builds you up rather than tears you down. It is phrased positively, in terms of what you want, not want you don't want. An example will show the difference.

"I don't want to get sick."
"I am healthy."

In the first example, you do not have an affirmation because it is worded for what you don't want instead of what you do want. This is very important because the mind does not recognize negatives. The mind works in pictures. When you describe what you don't want, the mind pictures it. What do you see when you say, "I don't want to get sick"? Most people see someone lying in bed—not a positive image. Now what happens when you say, "I am healthy"? Do you see someone well-toned and strong engaged in an outdoor sport or activity? As you are beginning to see, the two expressions seem to mean the same thing but are very different in the mind's eye.

When you create your affirmation, put it in the present tense, as if it has already occurred. This is a powerful technique for the mind, which does not know the difference between imagination and reality. It responds as if everything told to it in the present tense were true. Then, behavior begins to shift gently to align itself with the thoughts or beliefs. We want to use this capacity of the mind to get the outcomes we want with affirmations.

When you think negative thoughts, your mind uses this process to bring into reality negative outcomes. You may have heard this referred to as the self-fulfilling prophecy. For example, when you use negative thinking such as overgeneralization, you may say something like, "I never get promoted." With this message for the mind to work with, it goes about the process of bringing that statement into reality. Imagine the change if instead of saying, "I never get promoted" you began to say "I am successful." By putting it in the present tense, over time you will begin to behave as if you are successful, instead of behaving as if you will never get promoted. Remember, even things that are not yet true, if said positively and in the present tense, have a better chance of coming true than if you said them negatively. Affirmations mobilize the brain's capacity to create reality.

To be most effective, affirmations need to be said at least twice a day—morning and night—and more often, if you can remember to say them. When you say them to yourself, try to put as much feeling and emotion into them as you can. The mind listens more readily to emotion than to a dull monotone! If you doubt this, ask yourself if you'd rather listen to a dry, boring speaker, or an enthusiastic, excited speaker.

If you do this every day for a period of a few months, you will be amazed at how different you feel about yourself. A list of some possible stress management affirmations follows. Don't choose more than two or three to start. After you master them, you can add others.

I am calm and relaxed.
I manage my stress.
I manage my time.
I am confident.
I release all negative thoughts.
I calmly solve problems.

I'm getting better every day.
I feel at ease with myself.
I let go of irrational beliefs easily.

Daily Acknowledgments

As we end our days, too often we recount to ourselves all the things we did not do well. We recite the errors we made in speech, behavior, and judgement. This reinforces in our minds the exact behaviors we would like to reduce or eliminate. It makes us feel bad about ourselves and amounts to a systematic process of daily destruction.

Instead of reviewing your shortcomings, at the end of the day make a list of ten things about which you feel good. This does not need to be a list of major achievements, but simply a recounting of the day's activities and things that you thought went well. Kindnesses you showed, decisions you made, commitments you honored—anything you did that you think is positive goes on the list.

Like affirmations, if you begin daily acknowledgments today and use them over a period of a few months, you will be astonished at how your attention has shifted from failures to successes. You will also be amazed at how easily you can see your successes and how many more of them there are.

LET GO OF LOW SELF-ESTEEM

1. Affirm yourself (positive, present tense, daily)

2. Daily acknowledgment

Hurry Sickness

The person with low self-esteem who copes with it through achievement or productivity usually suffers from "hurry sickness." Such people discover that if they are able to do one task in an hour, a sense of accomplishment and good feelings about themselves result. They quickly figure out that if they could do *two* things instead of one in that same time period, they would feel even better about themselves. It works . . . for a while. Then they look for a bigger boost and try to do *three* things in that same amount of time. Now the threshold has been crossed. It may not be possible to do three things. They start to run late, they tense their bodies in the fight-or-flight response, and they create stress instead of good feelings. In an effort to "catch up," they put their life into "fast forward"—they walk fast, talk fast, eat fast, drive fast, anything to do more in less time. As this escalates, they develop "hurry sickness."

This disease creates stress for the people around the sufferer as well. As you increase the demands on yourself, you increase your expectations of others. The raised expectations are not always reasonable, and disappointments and frustrations can follow. We saw earlier in this chapter how irrational beliefs form demands instead of preferences. See if you recognize yourself or any of your colleagues in Linda.

Linda looked at her watch. The meeting was scheduled to start in a couple of minutes, but she decided to make one more phone call. Fifteen minutes later, she slipped into the meeting as discreetly as possible. Halfway through it, she excused herself to rush back to her office to meet with one of her staff members. She apologized for eating her lunch and for answering telephone calls during the conference. When the meeting was finished, she dashed over to accounting to get some final figures for a project. In the middle of her conversation with the accounting manager, she was paged and excused herself to hurry back to her office for her next appointment. The rest of the afternoon was just as hectic. At 5:00, she ran down the stairs rather than wait for the elevator, hoping she could beat the traffic out of the garage.

How does reading about Linda make you feel? Does it leave you out of breath and feeling frazzled yourself? Do you feel as if you are reading your own biography? Linda is suffering from hurry sickness. She does everything in a rush. Her life is filled with a constant sense of urgency. Consequently, she lives with a perpetual feeling of pressure and stress. She wishes she could ''calm down,'' but whenever she stops and tries to relax, she feels guilty, as if she ''should be doing something.'' Even her vacations are at this frantic pace. Last summer she went to Europe and saw seven cities in nine days.

Notice also, that Linda has begun to layer activities. This means she is trying to do two or more things at the same time. While she was having the supervisory conference, she ate lunch and took phone calls. How many of us have motioned someone to come into our offices and talk to us while we were busy writing a memo or drafting a report? How many times have we been on the phone and started talking to someone else? Do you try to complete your paperwork while attending meetings? Layer your clothes, don't layer your life!

How can you get off this treadmill? Start by becoming a better time manager. Go back to Chapter 2 and review the sections on scheduling and goal-setting. Practice saying "no." Then work on raising your self-esteem. When you feel okay about yourself, you can escape this deadly cycle of pushing to do more and more in less and less time. Give yourself some times when you can slow things down. Allow yourself to take some breaks. Give yourself permission *not* to accomplish anything. Chapter 5 will give you some suggestions about how to build breaks into your work. Why not stop right now and take two or three slow, deep breaths?

Competitiveness

A hallmark of the Type A personality is the competitive, driven lifestyle. Behind it, too, lie feelings of low self-esteem. Comparisons with others push us to "keep up" or "be better." All this serves the need to feel okay about ourselves.

For many Type As, competitiveness becomes an addiction manifested as workaholism. These people put in more and more hours, sometimes with fewer and fewer results. Other areas of their life suffer in consequence, and they feel guilty about this. "Quality time" has been a big boon for the Type A workaholics. Now they can justify the few minutes they spend with their families, children, and friends as "quality time."

Not all people who work long hours are workaholics. Peak performers experience work as play and a source of satisfaction. However, when it feels like a compulsion—when you feel driven by it—it has become an addiction.

Competitiveness is rewarded by this culture, which puts a premium on having, consuming, and doing. We have devalued being, cooperating, and contributing. Slowly, people are beginning to see the price they pay for this lifestyle in terms of their health and relationships with others. They are asking some difficult questions: Is the next rung on the ladder worth alienating my family, missing the childhood of my children, or risking triple-bypass surgery? Is a promotion worth uprooting my family to a new town, asking my spouse to leave his or her job, and abandoning friendships I've spent years cultivating?

Bob was the manager of research and development at a software firm. After years of 7-day workweeks in which 12-hour workdays were common, he decided the price was too high. He had gained weight and was all too aware that alcohol was his only way to relax enough to fall asleep. He decided it wasn't worth it anymore and quietly stepped down. He spent the next 4 months traveling, reading, and reflecting on his life. He wanted to discover for himself if there could be "life outside work."

When we pursue a competitive, driven lifestyle, we make choices based less on our values than on what other people will think. We choose careers that are "high paying" or offer advancement instead of careers that we love. We get caught up in "doing things right" instead of "doing the right thing." All this adds up to alienation from purpose, values, and meaning and consequently from ourselves. When we let go of these external pressures and take time for solitude, we get back in touch with ourselves. We can begin to answer the questions about what gives life meaning and purpose.

Aggressiveness and Hostility

The Type A tends to view life as a struggle. Consequently, they face each day, each person, and each situation as challenges to be overcome. Just winning is not enough for them; they want to dominate. Over time they invest ever-greater energy to fight ever-smaller battles. They upset themselves over small, unimportant matters. A veneer of anger and aggression is present in most of their activities. This hostility is a key predictor of heart attacks.

Many Type As are unaware of their ever-present hostility or are unwilling to admit it. In their minds, they are merely responding to situations. Isn't aggression appropriate when the photocopier doesn't work, when the person you want to call has a busy phone line, or when the computer doesn't do what you want it to do? This anger gets in their way of being able to accept situations for what they are, as described in Step 2 of our Model. Type Bs don't react to these minor inconveniences; Type As *over-*react. They would be wise to follow the advice of Nebraska cardiologist Robert Eliot.

1. Don't sweat the small stuff.

2. It's all small stuff.

3. When you can't fight and you can't flee, *flow.*

The competitiveness and aggression result in a person who is highly critical of everything. Such people tune in not to what is right or good in a situation, but what is wrong and what could be improved or made better. They cope with their feelings of low self-esteem by finding fault and expecting perfection. Their motto is, "We try harder."

You can reduce your stress and your risk of a heart attack by letting go of these Type A characteristics. Replace them with Type B qualities.

TYPE B BEHAVIOR

Type B people have several traits that distinguish them from Type A people. Instead of rushing all the time to do more in less time, they pace themselves and take breaks. They realize that a stretch break, a lunch break, or a vacation can result in increased productivity and better health.

Type B people also take time to enjoy the little things in life. They notice the exquisite sunrise as they drive into work in the morning. (The Type A person is pushing on the horn because someone is traveling at the speed limit in the left lane!) They stop and appreciate the extra effort a colleague put into a project, and they notice when the boss puts a new picture on her desk. Type B people do not become so focused on work that they lose sight of all the other dimensions of life.

You will hear laughter coming out of the office of a Type B person. Type As don't have time for such silliness; after all, life is *serious!* The Type B person takes time to read the funnies in the morning paper, while the Type A person reads the headlines and the business section. Meetings aren't all business; Type B people allow themselves to enjoy the job. This ability to see the lighter side helps the Type B person maintain perspective and balance.

Type Bs have a greater appreciation for the process of life, not just the outcomes. They understand that there is an ebb and flow—a time to work and a time to relax. They are not afraid to slow down and simply ''be.'' They understand the paradox that relaxation brings greater productivity, and they create escape hatches for themselves.

They fall victim to far fewer shoulds and consequently experience less anxiety and anger. They have fewer unrealistic expectations of themselves or others. Rather than carry around hostility, they ask for what they need and express their feelings. They actively use Step 1 of the CALM model—change the situation when you can—and also Step 2—accept what you cannot change. Type As, on the other hand, often fail to move to Step 2; they persist in a belief that they can change and control every situation, if only they exert enough effort. They confuse control with controlling.

Type Bs are not as likely to hold on or add on. They have learned to let go so that stress doesn't build. Rather than adapting to the stress, they are managing it.

Let Go of Type A Traits
Hurry sickness
Competitiveness
Anger and hostility
And Replace with Type B Traits
Take breaks
Enjoy little things
Laugh
Relax

SUMMARY

To maintain control of yourself and the stress you experience, you paradoxically will need to learn to let go rather than hold on or add on. Too often we hold on to the past, to things, to people, or to irrational beliefs. We add on pressures instead of setting limits. When we learn to let go, we have time to "be," to experience solitude and restore our balance. Without this ability, our lives become centered around doing, achieving, and accomplishing—all Type A traits. These traits are difficult to release because they have been valued in this culture. Yet we know we are at greater risk for a heart attack when we hurry, are competitive, and live with a veneer of hostility. Letting go gives us a healthier body and peace of mind.

5

The *M* of CALM: Manage Your Lifestyle and Make It Fun

When we notice we are under stress, we are faced with two choices. We can actively manage the stress, or we can try to cope with it. The first three steps of the CALM model have focused on how you manage the stressor and your response to it. The last step is designed to increase your overall resistance to those inevitable stressors through healthy lifestyle choices.

Despite our best efforts to change situations, accept what we can't change, and let go of our attachments, there still will be times when we experience stress. Building positive behaviors into your lifestyle will prepare you in advance to handle those inevitable days.

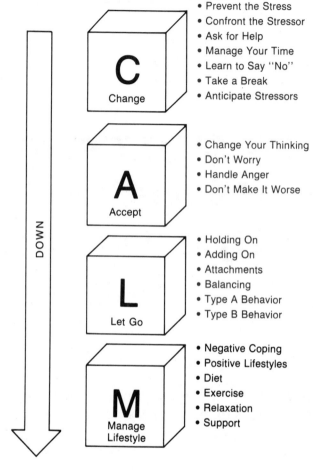

FIGURE 5.1

Notice that we say *positive* lifestyle behaviors. When most of us experience stress, we jump immediately into some type of coping. We don't stop to ask ourselves if we can change anything; we don't look at how we might be contributing to the stress through our thoughts, beliefs, or personalities; and we don't let go of stressors and accept what we can't change. Instead, we reach for something to reduce the feelings we have at the moment.

NEGATIVE COPING STRATEGIES

Unfortunately, many of our coping strategies result in additional stress. For example, alcohol is used widely to manage stress. Although one drink may help you relax and unwind from the day, two is not better. Look at what happened to Janet.

It was during the installation of a new computer system that Janet first started going out after work with "the gang" for a drink. In the beginning, she was the first to leave, usually after one drink. As the months progressed, though, and the job pressures continued, she stayed later and later. Eventually it became common for her to have three or more drinks. One night no one in the gang could stop for a drink. Janet found herself alone in the bar, wondering what had happened to her. She never would have thought she would be in a bar alone just to drink.

Drinking is not the only poorly chosen coping strategy. Others include eating, drugs, worry, blaming, smoking, spending binges, passivity, revenge, and aggressiveness. Each of these offers a "quick fix" but does not give you long-term relief from stress.

Short-Term Gain and Long-Term Pain

The problem with the preceding strategies is that they do work—for a little while. Perhaps after a particularly stressful week you feel you deserve a little reward and you take yourself shopping. When you buy something, you feel better, and you console yourself that the hard week was "worth it." The stress is reduced—until the following week, when you repeat the cycle. When this becomes a regular coping strategy, you have a house full of things you don't need or want, and you now may have a financial stressor in addition to your work stressors.

The process is the same with eating. Food becomes a reward or consolation for stress overload, and in a short time eating becomes overeating. Soon excess weight is another stressor and a health problem.

The difference between a stress management technique and a coping strategy is this: A coping strategy gives you short-term relief, but if you continue using that coping mechanism, over time you will have another problem. As we discuss the positive lifestyle behaviors, you will see the opposite effect. The longer the positive behaviors are used, the better you will feel and the more *resistant* you will become to stress buildup.

POSITIVE LIFESTYLE BEHAVIORS

The ultimate goal of stress management is to maintain health. Throughout the day, we face challenges and stressors that demand responses. The stronger and healthier the body, the more easily it can respond to those challenges and stressors. This can be graphically shown with force-field analysis. If you look at the left side of Figure 5.2, you will see some typical stressors you might encounter. They are pushing against the positive lifestyle behaviors on

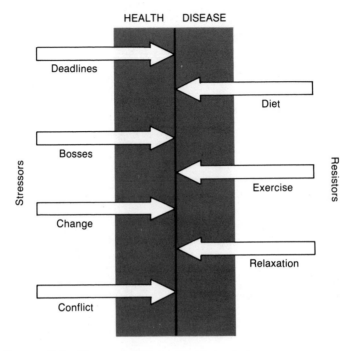

FIGURE 5.2   Stress and Force-Field Analysis

the right. As long as there is a balance between these, you stay healthy. However, if the stress increases or if your positive lifestyle behaviors decrease, you can cross into the area of disease easily.

The chart can be made more complete than what is shown here if you take into consideration the relative strength of the stressors and the resistors. Look at Figure 5.3 and notice how some stressor arrows cross into the disease column. The one resistor (friends) isn't strong enough to make it into the health column. This chart was prepared using Janet's

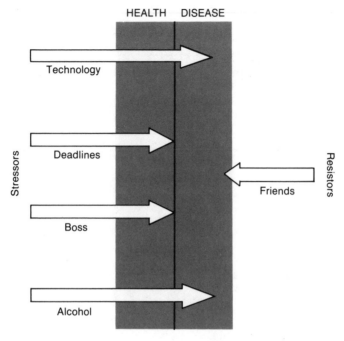

HEALTH   DISEASE

Technology

Stressors

Deadlines

Friends

Resistors

Boss

Alcohol

FIGURE 5.3   Stress and Force-Field Analysis: Weighted

case as an example. You will notice that her negative coper, alcohol, is included on the stressor side
of the chart. This is because the stronger a coper,
the more it puts you out of balance and leads you
toward disease rather than health. It might be helpful to think of copers as wolves in sheep's clothing!
If you hve an occasional drink, you would put alcohol on the left side with stressors, and your arrow
would stay within the shaded column for health. If
drinking has become a problem, as it has for Janet,
your arrow would move into the shaded disease
area.

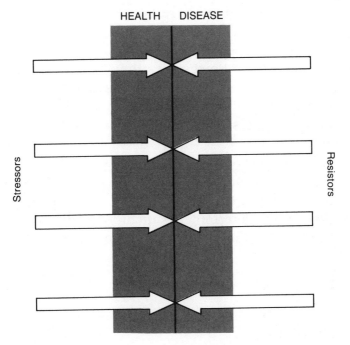

HEALTH   DISEASE

Stressors

Resistors

FIGURE 5.4   Stress and Force-Field Analysis: Worksheet

Figure 5.4 is a blank chart on which you can record your stressors and coping strategies. It gives you
an immediate graphic picture of what you need to
do to restore balance and maintain your health.

Positive lifestyle behaviors are not "quick fixes"
to be used when you feel stressed (for example, eating a salad rather than a hamburger for lunch does
not immediately reduce your stress). Instead, they
are the results of decisions you make about how to
live your life, the kinds of habits you are going to
maintain, and the value you assign to your health.
The more positive behaviors you integrate into your

lifestyle, the greater your resistance to stress. If you choose not to incorporate these positive behaviors into your life, you are still making lifestyle choices. Whatever your choices are, they will determine whether stress is a positive or a negative force in your life. The objective of stress management is not to eliminate stress, but rather to harness it for your benefit.

Do you *have to* change your lifestyle? No, there are no shoulds here. It is your choice. Just be sure you understand that your choices about how you live your life determine its quality and length!

Now, let's look at some of the positive lifestyle choices you can make.

DIET MAKES A DIFFERENCE

Collin got a late start this morning. As he dressed, he realized there wasn't time for breakfast. When he got into the office, he poured himself a cup of black coffee. At 10:30, when his stomach started to rumble, he walked to the vending machine and got a candy bar, which he ate with his third cup of coffee. He had an important sales call at 2:00 and worked through lunch to put the final touches on his presentation. At about 1:30 he noticed he was shaking, and he felt light-headed. He attributed it to nervousness and poured himself another cup of coffee to "calm his nerves."

Collin may have been nervous, but the symptoms he was experiencing were a direct result of his eating habits. We need to remember that food is the fuel that makes the body go. Without fuel, just like a car, it stops running. Using poor-quality fuel is equivalent to watering down the gas. There may not be a problem with the first tankful, but if you do that for a sustained period of time you're going to see poor performance.

Despite the variety of views on diet and nutrition, there are some accepted facts about the relationship between stress level and what we eat.

The Typical American Diet

Every country has its typical foods and traditional meals. Traditionally in the United States, breakfast consists of coffee, bacon, and eggs; lunch consists of a hamburger, fries, and soft drink; and dinner consists of meat and potatoes. Throughout the day we snack on doughnuts, candy bars, cookies, and chips. This diet worsens the effects of unmanaged stress, and for some people it can be lethal.

What's Wrong with the Typical American Diet

Let's start with coffee. It contains caffeine, an addictive substance that triggers the fight-or-flight response. We use caffeine as a stimulant in the morning and for the rest of the day. If we experience stress and the natural fight-or-flight response is also activated, our bodies are adapting to two stimulants. Then we wonder why we get the shakes and feel burned out!

Caffeine also is found in tea, chocolate, and a number of over-the-counter medications for pain relief, appetite suppression, and allergy control.

Consider reducing or eliminating caffeine from your diet. Limit coffee intake to one cup in the morning, then switch to water, fruit juice, herbal tea, or decaffeinated coffee. If you drink soft drinks, choose those without caffeine.

The second item in our American diet is bacon. This is followed by hamburger for lunch and meat for dinner. There is a lot of fat in red meat. We need some fat in the diet, probably about 30 to 35 percent of total calories, but most Americans consume closer to 45 percent of their calories in fat. The extra fat contributes to obesity and a high cholesterol level.

Cholesterol can clog the arteries, thereby causing heart attacks. The fight-or-flight response causes the heart to beat faster and pump more blood. If the arteries are clogged with cholesterol, and the blood can't get through, you increase your risk of a heart attack.

Consider cutting back your consumption of red meat and eating only meat that has been trimmed of fat. Have it fewer times per week, or consider using it as a side dish instead of a main course.

Egg yolks are also a major source of cholesterol. You can eat as many egg whites as you like, but try to limit your yolks to two per week. Consider eggs for breakfast a treat. Limit the traditional bacon-and-egg breakfast to once per week.

Bacon, fast-food hamburgers, fries, and many of our snack foods—especially chips—are loaded with salt. Sodium increases blood pressure and contributes to hypertension. Combine this with a high-cholesterol diet and Type A behavior and you have all the ingredients for heart disease. It's not surprising that more than half of all deaths in this country are from cardiovascular illnesses.

If you haven't done so already, take the salt shaker off the table! Do not add salt to your food without tasting it first. If you buy any processed foods, choose those labelled "low salt" or "low sodium." Get into the habit of reading the labels on the foods you buy. You may be surprised at how many foods list salt as one of the top two or three ingredients.

Most of our snack foods are loaded with either salt (for example, chips, nuts, pretzels, and crackers) or sugar (for example, doughnuts, candy bars, and cookies). Refined sugar contributes to harmful stress in three ways. First, its calories are empty. Our bodies do not get the fuel they need to perform at their best. Second, sugar gives the body a false high, that short-term gain we discussed earlier in this chapter, which is followed by a low. Third, sugar depletes the body of the vitamins it needs to counteract stress, especially B complex vitamins and vitamin C. These two vitamins are part of the body's natural defense strategy against stress. When sugar depletes the body of these vitamins, resistance is further lowered.

Why not choose snacks that are low in sugar and salt? Fresh fruit is an excellent alternative to "junk food."

If you are reducing caffeine, fat (cholesterol), salt, and sugar, you may be wondering what you are going to eat. Try fresh fruits, fresh vegetables, and whole grains. They give you a more balanced flow of energy as your body digests them, you feel full longer, and they help carry excess cholesterol out of the body. You will find these recommendations supported by both the American Cancer Society and the American Heart Association.

Don't try to make all these changes at once. Any dramatic change is more difficult to sustain than one that is gradual. You might start by reducing your salt intake. Notice how you feel. As you find yourself feeling better, it will be easy to try another change, and another, until you are eating more healthfully.

IMPROVE YOUR DIET

Decrease your intake of:
- Caffeine
- Fat (cholesterol)
- Salt
- Refined sugar

Increase your intake of:
- Fresh fruits
- Fresh vegetables
- Whole grains

EXERCISE: WHO NEEDS IT?

We all do! When you cope with angry customers, make difficult decisions under time pressure, manage stressed employees, and face traffic jams, you can spend the day in the fight-or-flight response. Unfortunately, you don't have the opportunity to run away from these pressures or fight anyone. Instead, you control that natural reaction, and by the end of the day you feel exhausted. If you don't relieve that built-up tension physically, you will discover that even a good night's sleep leaves you fatigued.

If you can hardly wait to get to the easy chair when you get home, and if you find yourself falling asleep in front of the TV at night, your body is telling you it needs to be exercised. Exercise or some form of movement will allow the body to rid itself of the accumulated physical responses to the day's stresses.

Benefits of Exercise

One key benefit of exercise is *energy.* Stress wears the body out, and exercise recharges it. Not only is there an increase in energy, but research studies consistently show that exercise improves mood. Literally "working out" our problems makes us feel better.

We also know that exercise slows the aging process and promotes better health as we age. The largest expense in this country is health care. With stress implicated in 75 percent of all illnesses, it becomes imperative that we each assume personal responsibility for our wellness. That is the only way we can reduce the nation's health-care bill. Responsibility for health is not something we can assign to someone else, trusting they will "fix" us no matter what.

Exercise tones the body. Cardiovascular fitness reduces the risk of heart attacks. The more the heart is used, the better it performs. It needs to be used regularly, though. Getting no exercise is better than getting hard exercise that is only sporadic.

How to Choose an Exercise Program

Many people wonder what form of exercise is "best." What is best is the exercise you will do regularly. Select something you enjoy, and do it at least three times a week. This could be swimming, jogging, bicycling, walking, or aerobics. Brisk walking is preferred by more people than any other form of exercise because it is enjoyable, convenient, and least likely to produce injury. If you haven't been in an exercise program until now, it can be a good idea to check with your family physician first. He or she may want to give you a stress test before recommending a particular program.

There is a caution for Type As. Because of their driving and competitive traits, many Type As approach their exercise programs as another conquest. They set the stopwatch as they begin their daily run and upset themselves if they don't better their previous best time. If you find yourself doing this, change to a less competitive activity, or stop yourself from measuring your performance.

In addition to all the other benefits listed, exercise can be the one time during the day that you can be alone. This is especially true if you are caring for a family in addition to working full time. Honor this time for yourself as much as you honor your company's working hours.

Exercises for the Desk-Bound

Do you live with a cat? If you do, you have a stress management teacher right in your own home. If you have spent any time around cats you know that they (like many humans) lead sedentary lives. However, there is one thing they do that we don't. They stretch. Have you ever noticed that when a cat gets up from a nap, it stretches its back and legs? Even if the "catnap" was only ten minutes long, the cat habitually stretches before moving on to the next activity. People who spend most of the day sitting at a desk encounter fatigue from the rigidity of their position. They need to think like cats and get in the habit of regular and frequent stretches. There are several exercises you can do at your desk to reduce stiffness and energize your body. Among the easiest are neck rolls and shoulder shrugs. We hold a tremendous amount of tension in the shoulders and neck. If you can get in the habit of doing this every hour, you will be amazed at the difference it can make. Begin by taking a few slow, deep breaths. Then bring your shoulders straight up and try to touch them to your ear lobes. Hold for a second or two, and then drop your shoulders. Do this three times. Do it right now as you're reading this book. Notice the difference?

Now drop your head gently to your chest, and lift it back up. Repeat this two more times. Now drop your head to your right shoulder. Keeping your shoulders down and relaxed, try to touch your ear to your shoulder. Repeat two more times. Then gently let your head fall backward, and bring it back up. Repeat this two times. Finally, drop your head to the left and try to touch your ear to your shoulder, keeping your shoulders relaxed.

The last step is to roll your shoulders forward a couple of times and then roll them backward a couple of times. Now you're ready to go back to your work. This takes only a couple of minutes to do and gives you a release from tension that would otherwise build.

Periodically, stand up and stretch. Reach your hands toward the ceiling, and then allow yourself to bend at the waist and hang limp like a rag doll. Do this two or three times. It also helps if you can take a couple minutes to walk, even if it is only to the drinking fountain.

If your legs become tired or cramped when you're sitting, lift them straight out, so they are parallel with the floor. Hold them out for a few seconds, and then relax them. Do this two or three times.

Millions of Americans suffer from lower back pain. This is caused by many things, including poor chair design, sloppy posture, and weak abdominal muscles. If you experience lower back pain and sit for extended periods of time, here are some tips. (See Chapter 8 for more suggestions.) First, be sure you are sitting straight in the chair with your lower back supported by the chair. When you lean forward to write or work on the keyboard, bend from your waist; don't lean by curving your back. Under your desk keep a large phone book or small box on which to rest your feet. There is less pressure on the lower back when your knees are level with or higher than your hips. Third, you can strengthen your abdominal muscles by sitting in your chair and doing some leg lifts. Put both hands on the seat of the chair to balance yourself. Pressing down with your hands and using your abdominal muscles, lift your feet about 6 inches off the floor. Hold this for a few seconds, and relax. Repeat this three or four times. This exercise can be done several times during the day, like the neck and shoulder exercises.

Do you notice yourself clenching your jaw? This is the cause of tension headaches for many people. You can relax your jaw by opening your mouth as wide as you can and sticking your tongue out. (Depending upon the situation, this also can be an excellent emotional release!)

Make a mental note or set a timer to remind you to stop and take a 2-minute stretch break every 55 to 60 minutes. It can reduce the tightness and soreness you feel at the end of the day.

RELAXATION

Exercise gives us a way to tone the body and release some of the tension that has built up during the day. Relaxation provides the body with a mechanism for preventing the buildup of tension in the first place. It is actually a process of letting go. You do not force your body to relax or push yourself to let go. Instead you allow it to happen. It's a lot like when you are trying to remember something; the harder you try, the less you can remember. However, as soon as you stop trying to force it, it magically comes to mind. With relaxation, when you notice yourself becoming tense or uptight, you release the tension by allowing your muscles to go soft instead of bracing them. Then, when you are relaxed and your muscles are supple, you are more able to "flow" with situations.

Diaphragmatic Breathing

The breath is the body's natural relaxer. When we exhale we let go of the breath, and as we do, the body is flooded with a feeling of relaxation. You may be thinking, "but that doesn't happen to me." Unfortunately, most of us no longer breathe properly and consequently do not experience relaxation as an outcome of our breath.

To get the relaxation benefits of the breath, we need to breathe diaphragmatically. Most of us are habitual chest breathers. In Chapter 1 we discussed the shift to shallow breathing from the chest as part of the fight-or-flight response. Because we experience so many little threats every day, we begin to hold our breath and rely on chest breathing. Diaphragmatic breathing begins to feel awkward and strange. To see if you are breathing diaphragmatically right now, place your left hand on your chest and your right hand on your abdomen, just below your navel. Now, notice which hand moves when you breathe. If your left hand moves, you are breathing from your chest. If your right hand moves, you are breathing diaphragmatically. Try to take your breaths from the diaphragm. One way to work on this is to use your stomach muscles to force your right hand to move in and out. This will give you a feeling for diaphragmatic breathing.

The easiest position in which to relearn proper breathing is lying on your back. In this position, it is difficult to breathe any way other than diphragmatically. Don't be surprised if something our bodies can do so naturally and effortlessly seems difficult at first. It is like any habit: Once we have been doing something a particular way for a long time, it begins to feel normal and right, even if it is incorrect. If you want to learn from real experts, watch small children breathe: Their stomachs balloon as they inhale and collapse as they exhale. The first step in being able to relax is to breathe diaphragmatically.

Progressive Relaxation

This form of relaxation, developed by Dr. E. Jacobson in 1938, focuses on muscle tension and uses a systematic process for tightening and releasing muscles. It is an excellent way to begin your training in relaxation, because you participate by doing something physical. Many other methods for inducing relaxation, some of which we will discuss on the following pages, use only your mental processes. Until you master progressive relaxation, you may find the other types more difficult.

This method is beneficial especially for people who need to use one group of muscles in their work and yet find themselves tensing many others. For example, you may sit at a terminal all day and use your hands for typing. Yet at the end of the day, your shoulders are sore and your jaw is clenched. Perhaps you write at your desk, using your hands and arms, yet you suffer from lower back pain. Progressive relaxation is a method that can help you learn to differentiate the various muscle groups and to tense only those that are actually needed for the task.

With prolonged practice, you can notice when you first start to tighten your muslces. At that moment, you can let go of the tension without ever allowing it to build. Most of us do not realize when we tense our muscles. The first clue is a sensation of pain.

In progressive relaxation, you systematically tighten and then relax the large muscle groups of the body—hands, arms, head, trunk, legs, and feet. This process results in muscles that are looser and more relaxed than before you started. After moving throughout the body, releasing all muscle tension, you open your eyes and are refreshed, alert, and ready to continue your day. Most people find it is helpful to have a voice guiding them through this process and will use an audiocassette. You can make your own tape or buy one commercially. Many bookstores carry them.

Meditation

Whereas progressive relaxation is a physical process, meditation is a mental process. Its goal is to calm the mind through focused attention on a word, phrase, or mantra. A widely recognized form of meditation is Transcendental Meditation (TM). When the mind is quiet, the body is also stilled.

Dr. Herbert Benson, a Harvard professor, in his well-known book, *The Relaxation Response,* describes the key elements necessary to induce the body into a state of deep relaxation. First you need a calm, peaceful, environment where you will not be disturbed. Turn your phone off or have someone else take your calls, and do not allow any interruptions. Second, you need a word or phrase you can use to focus your mind so it is not distracted by your usual thoughts. A calming phrase or a single word like "one," "peace," or "love" will work; use anything you can repeat silently to yourself. Third, you will assume an attitude of passive concentration. This means that if any thought does come into your mind, you gently let it go and refocus your attention on your chosen word or phrase. Finally, when you meditate, you want to be in a comfortable position. Most people find it is best to sit in a chair or recliner that supports the body, including the head. If you lie down, you may fall asleep. Like progressive relaxation, this process takes about 20 minutes and is recommended at least once a day, twice if possible. As meditation is practiced, the body learns to reach deeper and deeper states of relaxation.

Autogenic Training

This form of relaxation was developed by two European physicians, Dr. Schultz and Dr. Luthe. It is a type of self-hypnosis in which the body is given suggestions to regulate some of its "involuntary" functions. Like the other methods, there is a paradoxical effect that if you "try," you will not have success. With this technique you gain control when you give up control. You begin by getting into a comfortable position in a place where you will not be disturbed. Then repeat the following six instructions to yourself.

1. My hands and arms are heavy and warm (five times).

2. My legs and feet are heavy and warm (five times).

3. My abdomen is warm and comfortable (five times).

4. My breathing is deep and even (five times).

5. My heartbeat is calm and regular (five times).

6. My forehead is cool (five times).

You will have more success with this technique if you have already mastered progressive relaxation. As you gain experience with this technique, you will find you can complete it with only one repetition of the instructions rather than five. This is especially helpful to people with cold hands or feet and people with irregular heartbeats.

Guided Imagery

Often, imagery of a peaceful place such as a beach, forest, or mountain will be combined with some components of progressive relaxation. After a few minutes of deep, slow breathing, and after the body is quieting down into a state of relaxation, you imagine yourself in a peaceful setting where you can feel perfectly calm and relaxed. As you follow along with the imagery, your body responds as if it were actually there (think back to Chapter 3, in which we discussed how the mind treats thoughts as reality), often facilitating a state of deep relaxation. As you practice this technique, you will discover that in a stressful situation you need only picture your peaceful place, and your body will respond immediately with the relaxation response.

Many companies now produce prerecorded relaxation tapes. You can find them in bookstores and most record stores. Most combine soothing background music with progressive relaxation and guided imagery.

The Quieting Reflex

The benefit of regular practice of any of the relaxation techniques is that eventually you will be able to create that feeling with only one deep breath. Thus, when you face an irate customer, a conflict with your boss, or changing priorities you can resond with a calm, relaxed body instead of the fight-or-flight response. While relaxation can help calm you down, with practice it can become a primary preventive technique to avoid the stress reaction.

Dr. Charles Stroebel, in his book *QR: The Quieting Reflex,* outlines a 6-second technique you can use to activate the relaxation response anywhere, anytime. After you notice that you are in a stressful situation follow these steps:

1. *Say to yourself, "Alert mind, body calm."* For the stresses we experience in this culture we do not need to activate the fight-or-flight response. Instead, we need to activate our intellectual abilities, our communication skills, or our emotional resources. This step reminds

us we do not need to use our physical bodies for any of these tasks.

2. *Smile on the inside with your eyes and mouth.* This step helps reduce the tightening of the facial muscles and the jaw. By visualizing ourselves as smiling, we involuntarily relax the facial muscles.

3. *Take a deep breath, hold it, and exhale.* With the exhalations, let your body go limp with relaxation. Then go back to whatever you were doing. You can engage in the activity feeling calmer, clearer, and more relaxed.

The beauty of the technique is its simplicity. Stroebel advises you to use it often throughout the day—anytime you feel tension starting to build or notice any feelings of anxiety or a change in your breathing.

Biofeedback

Another method for learning to relax and let go of muscle tension is biofeedback. Use your local yellow pages to find a Certified Biofeedback instructor. He or she will use a machine to monitor your hand temperature, pulse rate, muscle tension, and sweat gland activity. All these are measures of the fight-or-flight stress response. After getting a baseline reading, the biofeedback instructor will teach you systematically the process of relaxation. The machine will provide you with immediate feedback on how deeply you are relaxing. This process usually takes several weeks to learn. Biofeedback is excellent for anyone suffering from migraine headaches, tension headaches, high or low blood pressure, cardiac arrhythmias, and Raynaud's disease.

SUPPORT

Emotional support can be a significant protection against stress buildup. It seems to work as a buffer between stress and health.

There are many types of support, including material, informational, and emotional. The most important of these for managing stress is emotional support—knowing that someone cares about you and is willing to listen to how you are feeling. Emotional support implies a trust between people that makes them willing to be vulnerable with one another. They will let go of the masks they may wear throughout the day and reveal who they really are—their hopes, fears, hurts, and joys. The caring from the supportive person has direct physical benefits. Students who watched a film of Mother Teresa, with her outpouring of love and support, were found to have stronger immune systems after the film than before. Support and love literally strengthen the body.

A helpful way to visualize this is to imagine a set of building blocks. Picture one block standing up vertically. That represents a person with a strong backbone! Now give that person wide shoulders for carrying heavy loads by placing another building block horizontally on the top of the first, so it is parallel with the ground. Now, begin piling the remaining blocks (representing stressors) on top of those broad shoulders. What is going to happen? It won't take too many blocks until the structure begins to wobble and falls over. So it is with people. We can carry only so much before we start to wobble and fall over. How could we strengthen the structure so it could carry more of those blocks? If you say add more vertical blocks to the base, you're right! If you put three or four blocks under the horizontal one, it will have a base strong enough to support the weight of many more blocks. The analogy applies to human beings. The more emotional support we have in our lives, the more stress we can manage.

Where can you find this type of support? You can find it everywhere! There may be someone in your company who can give you emotional support. You may get it outside the company from friends, family members, or neighbors. Sometimes you can find support from others in your profession, through your professional associations. Just about anyone has the potential to be a source of emotional support for you. If you have trouble developing these relationships, you can also find support through professionals, for example, social workers, psychologists, or counselors. There is no reason to be without this wonderful mechanism for handling stress.

When you choose people to fill this vital role for you, be sure you choose people who *can* support you. A person who tells you what you "should have done" is not being supportive, nor is someone who interrupts you to tell you his or her sad story. A constant giver of advice is not being supportive, nor is the person who tries to "fix" your problems.

When people support you, they listen to what you say without judging you. They accept your feelings, whatever they are. They do not give advice unless asked. They tell you the truth. They are willing to be available to you when you need them. They care about you as a person, and they believe in you. Do you have people like this in your life? If not, it may be time to find them. Take a moment now, and jot down the names of the people in your life who give you emotional support:

My sources of emotional support: _____

_____

Be careful that you don't count on only one person to meet all your emotional needs. This is easy to do and a dangerous practice. With only one person in this role, you risk needing support when he or she is sick, out of town, or caught up in a personal crisis. Then what will you do? It's as bad as if you have no one. Try to identify two or three people who can be a source of support.

Even when we have supportive people in our lives, we sometimes hesitate to use them, because we mistakenly believe that asking for help is a sign of weakness. To need a listening ear is to be dependent. To want to talk to someone means we are inadequate. Of course none of these statements is true; they are all irrational beliefs (see Chapter 4). In fact, it takes strength and high self-esteem to be able to ask for help. When you make this request, you are expressing a willingness to put yourself on the line, openly share your feelings, and risk being vulnerable.

Some of us are surrounded by people who can and do offer us support, but we consistently turn it down. We have difficulty accepting their support. We want to be perceived as "professional, competent, and together," never needy and never experiencing feelings of self-doubt or uncertainty. Paradoxically, this attitude projects an image of someone who is cold and inhuman, the opposite of what we really want. The "strong, together" professional recognizes the need for support and uses it. Support is part of what makes it possible to continue functioning at a high level, even during stressful times.

Emotional support can help us keep things in perspective, discharge negative feelings, and boost overall coping capabilities.

LAUGHTER

Type A people have difficulty taking time out to laugh. This is too bad for them and for their organizations, because laughter is healing and reduces stress. Remember the last time you had a really good laugh, the kind where your sides began to ache, tears flowed down your cheeks, and you begged the other person to stop? That kind of laughter puts your body into a profound state of relaxation, as when you throw a stone into the water, and you notice ripples radiating from the point where the stone hit. Laughter starts in your diaphragm, and ripples of relaxation flow out to the rest of your body. That's why you sometimes yawn after a good laugh; it's a signal that you are relaxed.

When you smile, you use fewer facial muscles than when you scowl or frown. A big smile can help release facial tension! Try smiling at people when you feel under stress; you will discover you feel better, they respond to you better, and your feelings begin to be more positive.

Norman Cousins, in his well-known book *Anatomy of an Illness,* describes his personal journey from terminal illness to health achieved through laughter. Not only does laughter buffer stress, it has healing properties. Consider how many of us have used the expression, "If I don't laugh, I'll have to cry."

Companies are beginning to recognize the positive effects of laughter, and many are seeking out the services of "humor consultants." These are people who look for ways the corporation can add fun to the work. When there is an atmosphere of enjoyment surrounding work, stress is lowered, people feel better, and productivity increases. For these reasons, humorists are frequently sought to speak at conventions to help establish a relaxed and fun atmosphere for learning.

There are several ways you can add humor to your workplace. One of the easiest is to bring a cartoon into the office and post it on a bulletin board. People seeing it will chuckle, and before long they will bring in their own favorite cartoons. You also can appoint someone within the office to provide "humor breaks." Most offices have someone with a natural ability to tell funny stories or jokes. Capitalize on this person's gift. In the process, others will learn to develop their own sense of humor. Another way is to look for what's funny in a situation. As we discussed in Chapter 1, you can decide how you will perceive a situation. Why not look for the humor instead of the pain? You can also create company "bloopers," which can be shared at meetings. You even can create your own "Blooper Hall of Fame." If you have a company newsletter, set aside some space for humor; it will probably be the most widely read column!

When you see something funny, let yourself laugh!

SLEEP

One of the fastest ways to create stress for people and make them crazy is to deprive them of sleep. You can cope with whatever stresses you are experiencing more effectively if you are rested. We all know how much sleep we need to feel good and be effective. Whether it is 6 hours or 8, protect that time. If you find yourself unable to get enough sleep, the daily use of 20 minutes for deep relaxation as described previously can compensate for some of the loss.

SUMMARY

When we experience stress, our first reaction often is to try to reduce or alleviate the tension we feel by using a short-term coper. As we have seen, copers like alcohol, eating, spending money, or smoking make us feel better for the moment, but over a longer period of time become additional stressors.

Instead of merely coping, we want to increase resistance to stress by managing our lifestyles. Specifically, we want to eat nutritious foods that allow us to function at our peaks. We want to keep our bodies strong and healthy through regular exercise. We also want to learn to short-circuit the fight-or-flight response through the regular use of relaxation techniques. When we do find ourselves in stressful situations, we want to take advantage of emotional support, laugh when we can, and get enough rest.

None of these techniques will get at the *cause* of stress; that was covered in the previous steps of the model. This final step is designed to make us as resistant to stress as is possible.

Part III

APPLY THE
MODEL

6

I Don't Like My Job

When Dave started in Customer Service at the car dealership, he was excited about working with people. However, that was before he knew what it was like to deal with customer complaints all day long. That was also before he knew that management would not stand behind the decisions he made.

Four years later he had an ulcer, checked his blood pressure at the machine in the grocery store every time he shopped, wouldn't talk to his wife until after his second drink, and dreaded going to work.

Family and friends tried to get him to quit. "Try something different," they urged. Every time Dave was ready to resign, though, the dealership came through with a raise or some perk. He tried to convince himself it was worth it to stay. When he finally realized that not only was he miserable, but he was making his wife miserable, he took the risk and quit.

He changed professions, took a cut in pay, regained his health, and restored his marriage. Today Dave will tell you leaving the dealership was one of the best decisions he ever made. In addition, today his income far exceeds what he left behind.

Many people are currently in jobs they don't like. This chronic dissatisfaction results in stress and a myriad of symptoms (Chapter 1).

How satisfied are you with your work?

Sadly, many of us choose a field of work based on other people's expectations and not on what we really want to do. Or when we're young, because we need to "declare a major," we pick something—anything—before we have had the time to find out what is in our hearts and before we know what we want to do. Then we awaken one day to the awareness that we're not happy; we do not enjoy what we do. We may feel "burned out." Friends and family are astounded that we could dislike doing what we are so good at. How could we consider leaving jobs in which we have good benefits and a good salary?

It is difficult enough to acknowledge to ourselves that the work we do is not personally satisfying. It is even more difficult to act on that knowledge.

SECURITY OR FULFILLMENT?

Chris didn't know exactly what she wanted to major in while she was in college. She was good in math, and her counselor advised her to go into computers. She was told she could make a good income and that lots of jobs were available. Chris was quick to learn about computers, and when she graduated, she got a job with the data processing department in a bank. Then the headaches started. At first, they were just dull aches, but over time she began to suffer from migraines. This went on for a period of years, until she finally noticed a pattern. Her migraines seemed to occur on weekends, holidays, and vacations—whenever she wasn't working. When she recognized this, she was forced to admit that she did not like her work. The company was great, her colleagues were fine, she just didn't like working on the computer all day. She wanted to make a change and get into some other line of business. However, she would be a candidate for a promotion in just another 6 months, and she was close to being vested in the retirement program. Besides, where else could she make that kind of money?

What would you do in Chris's situation? The symptoms our bodies experience when we are under stress are its gentle way of saying, "Pay attention—something is not right here." When we don't heed the gentle message, our bodies turn up the volume. Chris began with dull headaches; now she has migraines. What will it take to get her to listen? Right now, she medicates the symptoms so that she can continue to be productive on the job. Millions of people do this every day with tranquilizers, alcohol, or other drugs. This doesn't solve the problem, and it is only a matter of time before the body rebels again with a new or intensified symptom.

Instead of masking her symptoms with medication, Chris could take the time to listen to the message her body is sending her. It is not too difficult to hear if we are willing to listen. The problem is, we seldom like what we hear. Too often, it puts us into internal conflict with our values. Chris is caught between security and self-fulfillment. Which is more important? Each of us will need to answer the question for ourselves. Chris's body says security has a high price. What she needs to explore is whether there is a way to experience security *and* self-fulfillment.

If you are unhappy with your present work, the rest of this chapter will outline a process you can use to gain greater clarity about what you really want to do. Sometimes we need to change careers, and sometimes we need to revitalize the work we are doing at the moment.

IDENTIFY YOUR PASSION

The process starts inside yourself, not externally with the job market or your skills. Starting from the outside and working in—as most people do—is a source of stress. You meet other people's needs instead of your own. Working from the inside out requires more courage and a willingness to risk. It is also the path that will connect you with your purpose. People need and want meaningful work. Sadly, many of today's white-collar office workers feel as disconnected from the meaning of their work as blue-collar factory workers did in the past. Consequently, as Yankelovich discussed in his book *New Rules,* more and more of us are seeking fulfillment from our jobs. Perhaps this explains why there are more new businesses starting up now than ever before. People are beginning to take responsibility for their need for meaningful work.

To find work that you will enjoy, the first questions you need to ask yourself are: "What do I *want* to do?" "What excites me?" "What do I feel passionate about?" These questions can help you identify an intangible, internal magnet that will draw you toward itself. Others have referred to this as a "calling," a "vocation," the "music within," or "following your bliss." We'll use the word "passion" here because it literally says it all. Look at the word carefully and you see Pass-I-On. That's what meaningful work is all about. It is your ability to give of yourself through your contribution and service. Each of us has a unique contribution to make. When you are aligned with that purpose, you experience less stress than when you aren't.

Take some time right now to think about *your* passion. At this point you do not want to censor anything. Give all your thoughts equal consideration. There is plenty of time to play critic later. Don't be surprised if you come up with a big question mark: What *is* my passion? To know your passion requires that you have some time to stop and reflect. We get so busy at times that we forget to stop and take any personal time alone to think about what we want. If you begin to take time each day for relaxation or meditation as recommended in Chapter 5, you will find that answers to this question begin to bubble up and make themselves known to you.

Another reason we have trouble answering this question is that we spend too much time worrying about "what other people will think." Consequently, no sooner does a thought present itself than we begin to look at it through our spouses' eyes, our parents' eyes, our friends' eyes, and so on. If we anticipate rejection or a challenge from any of these sources, we discount the thought almost before it fully emerges.

There are two fears that hide our passions from us. First, our passions are hidden because our energies are poured into avoiding what we don't want rather than striving for what we do want. Take Murray for example. He has spent the past 20 years trying to avoid poverty. He has built a successful business in the process, but he feels driven in his work. No matter how well he is doing, he fears that the next quarter his luck may turn. Therefore, he feels an imminent sense of gloom and worries all the time. He suffers from ulcers and, despite his external successes, doesn't feel happy with his work or lifestyle. If Murray were following his passion, he would create his business around what he wants, not what he hopes to avoid.

Second, you may know what you want to do, but you are afraid of the risks. You lack the courage to go forward with your passion. Risk is a funny thing. It only appears that way from the outside—outside of commitment, that is. When you make a commitment to yourself to follow your passion, then you begin to carefully study how you can convert your dream into reality. This might be better called "calculated risk taking." From this perspective, it does not feel risky. As Goethe said, "The moment one definitely commits oneself, then providence moves too. All sorts of things occur to help one that would never otherwise have occurred. A whole stream of events issues from the decision, raising in one's favor all manner of unforeseen incidents and meetings and material assistance which no man could have dreamed would have come his way."[1] Don't let fear keep you from seeing what it is you really want to do.

We also fail to explore our passions because we think we aren't good enough, smart enough, or educated enough, or _____ enough. You can fill in the blank with any word you want. The point is, your self-esteem is slipping. We have already seen that low self-esteem is the source of many traits that create stress for us. Now we see that not liking or believing in ourselves can prevent us from being willing to go after what we feel will be meaningful work. The truth is, if you feel a passion inside yourself, you can begin to bring it into reality right now. That is not to say you won't need to start with small steps. However, you don't need to have everything "perfect" before you start. You are okay right now, the way you are.

If you think low self-esteem is keeping you in a job that is unfulfilling, go back to Chapter 4 and practice the ideas given there for how to raise your self-esteem.

Finally, our passions hide behind the dollar sign. Of course, we all need an income to be able to manage in this society. Too often, though, the dollar sign becomes the reason for doing or not doing something. Chris suffers headaches because money (security) is more important to her than health. Is it, though? We fail to remember that money is the reward that comes from unique service to others. Money is not the goal. This confusion that exists in so many people's minds has resulted in an ever more competitive culture in which "success" is measured in dollars and cents. Jennifer James in *Success is the Quality of Your Journey* says it well: "Remember,

168 III **Apply the Model**

when you can, that the definition of success has changed. It is not only survival, the having—it is the quality of every moment of your life, the being. Success is not a destination, a place you can ever get to; it is the quality of the journey."[2]

You begin the process of finding more satisfying work by looking inside and seeing what you feel drawn to do. Once this step has been completed—and it may take some time—you can move forward with more conventional career planning.

Now you can look at the kinds of work that would allow you to fulfill your passion. You can consider what companies specifically will provide you with the best environment for using your skills. You can begin to think about the kinds of people you want to work with. Don't be seduced by your talents. Because you are good with numbers, as Chris was, doesn't mean you will necessarily enjoy working with them. Because you were trained as a lawyer doesn't mean you will enjoy practicing law. Take Dennis, for example.

Dennis had always had a "good head" for business, and when he graduated from college his first job was with a mortgage company. Over the years he experienced a series of promotions and so stayed with the company. At age forty, he looked at his life and saw that he was a mortgage lender by default. It was a career he had fallen into, not one he had chosen, and it bored him much of the time. That boredom translated into a generalized feeling of fatigue that he fought nearly every day. When he asked himself what he really wanted to do and what he felt passionate about, he knew in a moment that he wanted to run a hardware store. Will Dennis be able to let go of his high-paying position to follow his passion? He is already taking some small steps. He has noticed that whenever he thinks about the hardware store or takes any action in that direction, his energy level immediately increases. So, he has started to plan ways to involve himself in the hardware business.

When you become clear about your personal mission, you don't necessarily walk into your boss's office and hand him your resignation! Identification is only the first step in the process. At this step you look inward for your personal purpose. Once this is done, you can move on to planning and goal setting, informational interviewing, resume writing, and market analysis. Each stage is important, and the order is critical. Throughout this process, you can use the CALM model to manage your stress. Let's see how Dennis can apply the model while he works on ways to open a hardware store.

CAREER CHANGE AND THE CALM MODEL

Change the Situation

Dennis can begin by asking himself what parts of his job currently give him the most satisfaction. Is there any way he can increase the amount of time he spends in these areas? This can make it less stressful for him while he is exploring options for what he really wants to do. He also can make a decision that he will take action to change his work while recognizing that it may take some time.

Accept What Can't Be Changed

Although Dennis wants to open his own hardware business, he needs to accept his current situation. He can monitor his thoughts for how they may be contributing to his stress. He can shift his focus from how much he dislikes his work to watching for things he can learn that will help him in his next venture. Remember that everything we do prepares us for the next step. Many of the things Dennis has learned about business as a mortgage lender can help him as he plans for his own business. Some of the people he has helped with loans may be able to help him in his new venture. It will not be productive for him to worry, either about his present situation or whether things will work out with the hardware store. Instead, he needs to take action to collect the information he needs to make decisions. One key will be to write out affirmations for himself to keep his mind filled with the positive things he wants. That way, there is less room for the negative fears that can trap him into only avoiding what he doesn't want.

Let Go

Dennis will also need to pay attention to his belief systems. Does he believe he deserves to do what he wants? Does he have the right to experiment with a new career direction? Can he risk not knowing everything and making some mistakes? He will need to let go of some security to be able to reach out for the new opportunities.

His level of self-esteem will have an impact on the confidence he feels as he pursues a new direction. Low self-esteem and Type A behavior mean he will demand more of himself and be less able to accept that career change takes time. Patience is a virtue that can reduce the stress.

Manage Your Lifestyle and Make It Fun

It is important that Dennis doesn't take himself too seriously. Although changing a career is important, it can also be fun! During the process, Dennis will need some support. This can come from friends or a career counselor. These people can be a sounding board for him as he sorts out his ideas.

Seeing that his body is well-cared for during the transition can help with the fatigue Dennis has been experiencing. He has had some difficulties sleeping at night that are caused in part by his sedentary lifestyle. By starting a regular exercise regimen, he will have more energy, sleep better, and awaken more refreshed. Just as he is in a vicious circle now, he can catapult out of it by taking steps toward a healthier lifestyle. Dennis is not asking himself to adjust to an unpleasant situation. He is asking himself to manage his stress while he puts a new plan in place. This knowledge can be freeing to him and release creative energy.

He also will want to take time to relax and have solitude. This will help him physically, and it will give him the private time he needs to reflect on what it is he really wants to do. When he invests this time, the how will become more clear.

In summary, we see that Dennis needs to focus on the first and fourth steps of the model. He needs to take some steps to change his situation. His dissatisfaction with his work rather than his thoughts or behavior is creating the stress. In the interim, while he develops his plan, he needs to develop more positive lifestyle behaviors that can reduce or eliminate the symptoms he is experiencing.

If Dennis does not put meaning back into his work, he is headed for burnout. It is not long hours that burn you out, contrary to what many people think, but rather long hours of *meaningless* work. "Burned out people have lost their sense of purpose; their work no longer matters to them."[3]

REVITALIZE YOUR JOB

Is finding a new job the only way to overcome feelings of dissatisfaction with your work? "Many times it is not the nature of the job itself, but the inner baggage of negative and limiting beliefs and expectations, that turns off the energy and excitement you could have at work."[4] In these situations you need to revitalize your present job.

- Look at your expectations. Are they realistic?
- Look at your attitudes. Are you confusing mistakes with failures? Mistakes are learning opportunities; failures are self-esteem killers.
- At what point in your life cycle are you? In our early years we focus on our competence, which

is outer-directed. After we master a set of skills, the focus becomes more inner-directed as we concern ourselves with meaning and service. Going through this transition does not mean you need to change jobs; it means you need to find meaning in your competencies.

· Don't always play it so safe. Take a risk, and make a difference in your company. Remember, it is sometimes easier to ask forgiveness than permission.

· Start small. Change takes some time. Try out a new idea in a small corner of your life. If it doesn't work, you can try something else. It is not necessary to revolutionize your life!

· Try job enrichment. Look for ways that you can expand the job to make it more meaningful. Don't expect that this is your boss's job or the human resources department's job. *You* are responsible for your career and whether or not it is meaningful to you.

SUMMARY

If you don't like your job, there is something you can do about it! Either you can change jobs or you can revitalize the job you have. The first step is to take some time with yourself to reflect on what you really want. What will give your work meaning? As you look for the answer to this question use the CALM model to manage the stress during the transition.

REFERENCES

1. Quoted in Roy Rowan, *The Intuitive Manager,* (Boston, MA: Little, Brown and Company, 1986), 53.
2. Jennifer James, *Success Is the Quality of Your Journey,* (New York: Newmarket Press, 1983), 3.
3. Dennis T. Jaffe and Cynthia D. Scott, *Take This Job and Love It* (New York: Simon and Schuster, Inc., 1988), 67.
4. Ibid., 127.

7

My Stressor Works at the Next Desk

There was no doubt that Steve was bright. He was a quick thinker and articulate. For these reasons, he was an asset to the team. When it came to getting along with others, though, he seemed totally incompetent. There was something about the way he asked a question that made you feel you were on trial. Because he was so bright, he found the flaw in any suggestion. That would have been okay, if he didn't tell you with words dripping with judgement. Howard didn't know what to do. He loved his work, and he liked most of the people he worked with. Whenever he had contact with Steve, though, his stomach wound up in knots.

When you like the people you work with, almost any stressor is easier to handle. However, if your work environment is negative, and you feel distrustful of fellow employees, a relatively insignificant stressor may be sufficient to upset you.

The rest of this chapter will give you some ideas about how to turn a negative work environment into one that is more positive.

PEOPLE ARE DIFFERENT

Have you ever noticed how the world is divided into fours? There are four seasons, four food groups, four directions . . . and four kinds of people. Once you learn to identify each type, you can adjust your communication to reduce conflicts and increase your interpersonal effectiveness. The four types have been given many different names. For our purposes, we will call them *Direct, People-oriented, Detailed,* and *Supporters.*

Directs are assertive, sometimes even blunt. They have a "take charge" attitude that at times is perceived as arrogance. They like change and see it as challenging. Therefore, they initiate changes and make things happen. Like the Type As, these people are impatient and frequently suffer from hurry sickness.

The second group is *People-oriented.* They enjoy talking with people, working with people, and being around people. They tend to be warm and outgoing and can make you feel at ease almost immediately. Because they stay in touch with people, they often have a good sense of the emotional climate in an organization. They "read" what people say as well as what they don't say. People-oriented types don't like to be bothered with details; they like to get a "feel for things."

Our third group is *Detailed*. They pay attention to detail, and they often are perceived as perfectionists because they want things done "right." They are analytical; they weigh pros and cons before they make a decision. Unlike the Directs or People-orienteds, they are reserved and prefer to respond rather than initiate.

The last group is *Supporters*. They follow through on projects and see that things get done. Like the Detaileds, they are more reserved in their interactions with people, often waiting for someone else to open a conversation. However, once they get to know you, they can be quite warm and friendly. These people tend to support the status quo, therefore they need time to adapt to changes. They have a stabilizing effect on an organization.

Which type are you? Remember, one type is not better than another. Each has a role to play in an organization, but because of differences in how each approaches the world, there can be conflicts among the various types.

For example, imagine you are a Direct working with a Detailed. As a Direct, you would like quick answers and new ideas. The Detailed person will give you more information than you want and will want time to carefully review and consider proposed changes before acting on them. This can be frustrating. On the other hand, if you are the Detailed person, it is equally frustrating to talk to someone who tries to finish your sentences for you and seems to make impulsive decisions. The challenge is to value each person's perspective so that the overall outcome is positive.

What if a People-oriented is working with a Supporter type? The more reserved Supporter may feel
the People-oriented is coming on too strong. If this
happens, there can be feelings of distrust. Because
the Supporter follows through on things, there can
be frustration or anger when the People-oriented
type doesn't pay much attention to the details. The
People-oriented wonders why the Supporter seems
so cautious and always wants time to think before
making a decision. With any combination of styles,
there is the potential for conflict. Look what happened to Lynn.

Lynn had been working for the same insurance
agency for 12 years. She loved her work and was
successful. Because she had been there longer than
any other agent, she often was consulted and over
the years became an informal boss. That all changed
when Crystal was hired. Crystal, like Lynn, was a
Direct and didn't like consulting someone else. She
quoted policies the way she wanted and answered
customers' technical questions without asking
Lynn's advice.

Although irritated, Lynn could handle this. However, Crystal got "under her skin" when she
chastised the other agents for seeking Lynn's advice.
Over a period of 3 months, Lynn developed a terrible skin rash that even the doctor couldn't get under control. The office split into two camps, and
Lynn began to think of quitting.

What happened? Both Directs, Lynn and Crystal
each wanted to be in control. Their power struggle
created an unhealthy emotional climate for themselves and the other people in the office. Rather than
fighting with each other, they needed to CALM
down and figure out how to work together.

If an organization were staffed with only Directs, there would be constant fighting over who was in control. If it were filled with People-orienteds, it would be more of a social club than a workplace! If there were only Detaileds, their perfectionism might prevent them from ever getting anything done. If it were all Supporters, the organization would not grow and take risks, but would become stuck in the status quo. So, you see, your organization needs people to be different. That is the way it can grow and thrive.

Follow these tips when you deal with the different types:

Directs. Get to the point; they like the bottom-line. Don't criticize them; they tend to have high egos. Don't try to control them; they like to have the authority.

People-orienteds. Establish a relationship first. Before you do business, nurture the relationship. Don't ask them to deal with details. Keep things as positive as possible.

Detaileds. Give them time to study the facts. Go slow; allow them to ask questions. Provide them with background information. Don't put them on the spot in a group setting.

Supporters. Take time to break the ice before you start your business. Give them time to adjust to changes; plan changes. Give them time to think before asking them to act. Give them sincere recognition for a job well done.

To manage stress, we need to accept people who are different. If we try to make them like us, or if we judge them, we only create stress for ourselves.

To solve today's complex problems, we need a variety of points of view. There is not one simple solution. There is not one "right" way. If we don't recognize differences as a gift, we can miss some real opportunities.

DEALING WITH DIFFICULT PEOPLE

Each of us does the best we can to get our needs met. Some of us have better skills than others. The more skills we have, the easier we are to get along with. People who are limited to only a few basic skills are often perceived as "difficult."

Paula had worked in the marketing department for 8 years. Over the past 3 years, ever since Eric became manager, morale had steadily declined. Paula was so frustrated she was updating her resume. Eric agreed to every request made by the marketing staff and followed through on none of them. They didn't have the supplies they needed and couldn't get approval to attend important conferences; worst of all, decisions were never made. Paula often wondered why Eric wouldn't do his job.

What can we do with difficult people like Eric? First, let go of any feelings of anger. It will not change these people or make the situation better. Anger will only upset you and depress your body's immune system.

Second, let go of the notion that you need to like everyone you work with. You don't. You need a business relationship that allows you to get the job done. It would be nice if you liked everyone, but it is not necessary.

Third, let go of any fantasies you have that you can change others. The only person you can change is yourself. If you begin to respond differently to the difficult people in your life, they may respond differently to you. To change yourself with the goal of changing others is manipulative and will be seen as such by other people. They won't change in response to this kind of behavior on your part. Change yourself to please yourself, not in hopes of making someone else different.

Fourth, *listen* to these people. They have some need they are trying to express, however ineffectively. See if you can understand what their real concern is. Show some compassion. Haven't you at some time felt powerless and used ineffective communication? Most of us have. Rather than trying to get them to stop their behavior by controlling them, try instead to empower them.

We all think we know how to listen, but few of us really do. Start by giving other people your attention. Put down the paper you were reading or the memo you were writing. Look them in the eye. Now watch their faces for their expressions as they speak. Watch their gestures, and notice if they agree or disagree with their words. Listen to their words. Don't stop there; use your mind to understand the meaning of those words. Use your feelings to understand their feelings. Are they upset about what they're telling you? Excited? Disappointed? As you can see, this is an active process. It takes concentration, commitment, and effort.

After you have listened to another person, check to see if what you understand is what he or she meant. Do this *before* you respond. If you do not understand, it is useless for you to try and make your point. You will not have communication, which is a dialogue. Instead, you will have two monologues. If you make a promise to yourself not to express your opinion until you understand the other party, you will eliminate at least half your disagreements with people, becaue half the time people disagree they simply misunderstand each other.

The other half the time, you will discover that even disagreement is acceptable when you feel you have been heard. When we don't feel other people are listening to us, the natural tendency is to do something to try to get their attention. This might be to speak louder or become more aggressive or argumentative. In most instances, communication deteriorates, conflict escalates, and stress results.

Listening pays dividends when you're dealing with difficult people!

Fifth, if you notice there are many difficult people in your life, maybe you need to look *inward* instead of outward. When we are not managing stress and become burned out, it is not unusual for us to see others in a negative light. Under these circumstances, a boss who makes a request is "demanding," a supervisor who wants completed work is "unreasonable," and a colleague who asks for information is "picky." The meanings we're attaching to these situations are based on our point-of-view, not based on reality. Don't be too quick to point your finger at others as being difficult, because you may see three of your fingers pointing back at you!

Finally, before you say anything to a difficult person, ask yourself this question: "Is what I am about to say going to affirm or diminish this person?" If it will diminish the person, close your mouth and don't speak. To knowingly attack another's self-esteem is to lower your own.

Remember—when you are having a great day, people seem friendly and helpful. When you are having a bad day, though, people seem rude or indifferent. The only difference in these situations is your thinking and your attitude. You can control how you react to people.

You control yourself, your thoughts, and your reactions. You let other people upset you. You give your power away to so-called "difficult" people. As we've said throughout this book, control is critical to managing stress. Be in charge of deciding if someone is going to upset you.

SUMMARY

Often our stress is associated with people with whom we work on a day-to-day basis. To CALM down, remember that although we can change the situation, we cannot change other people. Instead, we need to accept that people are different and use those differences to get the job done. Instead of judging others, which can only diminish their self-esteem and upset us, affirm them for their differences. Then, let go of your expectations that people be like you. Let go of any illusions you hold that you can control others. We are all doing the best we can. Some of us have more skills and some of us have fewer skills than others. If we can't control others, we still can manage our stress (and have fun) when we choose to control our reactions to the people in our offices.

8

On the Road Again . . . and Feeling Stressed

Lester had been travelling for years. He was a university professor and professional public speaker. It was not uncommon for him to teach a class in the morning, catch a plane that afternoon, speak at a dinner meeting, and fly the last plane home that night. He knew the pace was hectic, and he often pushed himself even when he was tired. Many times he regretted having said "yes" to one speech or another. He began to wish he could get off the treadmill, but he wasn't able to say "no" when he was asked to speak, even if it meant flying the red eye to be back in time to teach his classes at the university.

As the years passed, he became increasingly fatigued, until one day as he boarded the plane he felt a wave of panic rush over him. He broke into a cold sweat, and all the color drained from his face. As the plane doors closed, he felt the walls closing in on him. He felt trapped. For the first time in his life, Lester felt afraid of flying.

The stress of travelling caught up with Lester, and he was experiencing what many veteran travellers know as "flying phobia." This is how some frequent fliers may experience burnout. Burnout is the body's way of saying, "no more, I've had it." For most of us, when our bodies finally break down, we stop, reevaluate what we're doing, and often make lifestyle changes. For the frequent traveller, flying phobia serves the same purpose. It is extremely difficult to continue travelling when the thought of being on a plane results in an anxiety attack. Some people, of course, do continue to travel despite the extreme discomfort, in the same way that some Type As maintain their frenetic pace even after bypass surgery.

Why do people get burned out on the road? Probably the single biggest reason is the ongoing lack of control. Throughout this book, we have emphasized the importance of a sense of control. That feeling of being in charge of ourselves, no matter how small, overrides feelings of powerlessness. When you're on the road, feelings of powerlessness are common from the minute you start your day until you go to bed at night. Let's look at just a few of the situations over which you don't have control.

1. If your flight isn't booked well in advance, you may not have a choice of where you sit on the plane.

2. Air traffic controllers, mechanics, airline personnel, the weather, and other flights determine if your flight will be on schedule—you don't.

3. On flights longer than 2 hours, you cannot choose a smoke-free environment even though you sit in the "nonsmoking" section.

4. You cannot always control when or what you will eat.

5. You cannot choose your room furnishings, or even the type of pillow you sleep on.

6. Your exercise program may not be on your preferred schedule, or you may not be able to participate in your regular activity.

7. You cannot share a meal with a spouse or friend if you want to.

8. You do not control how quiet or noisy your environment is.

This is just the beginning! Is it any wonder that many travellers come home feeling exhausted and say they need at least a day to recover from the stress of being gone?

You do have some options. There are things you can do to gain a greater sense of control in this situation. Let's take a look at them.

FLYING

You do not know when a flight will be delayed or cancelled, whether owing to mechanical problems, weather conditions, or air traffic. Therefore, you will experience less stress if you do *not* take the last flight to your destination. Leave yourself the option of another, later flight if something happens to yours. Then, if you learn your flight is cancelled, you won't panic about how to reach your destination.

If you travel with any frequency, carry a copy of the OAG (Official Airline Guide). It lists all the flights and flight times. If you are delayed, it gives you a quick reference for other available flights. You also may want to carry back-up flight information as a matter of routine. Then, if you experience a cancellation or delay, you already have the information about the next flight available. You can ask your travel agent to tell you in advance how many seats are available for your back-up flight.

If your flight is cancelled, and the gate agent is making changes, get out of the line and go to the nearest phone. If you use a reputable travel agent, they will provide you with a 24-hour toll-free number. Call them and let them book your new flight. It will save you time and frustration.

Also, give serious consideration to joining the airline club of the carrier you use most frequently. In the event of a delay, such a club will help you with your change of flights, and the club provides you with a more relaxed environment for waiting. You also will find it is a welcome respite when you have a long layover between connections. When you are on the main floor, the physical environment with its crowding, announcements, beeping motorized carts, and uncomfortable chairs contributes to the stress you feel. The airline club provides comfortable chairs, quiet background music, usually fewer people, and a professional staff to serve you. It doesn't require many trips to recover your financial investment.

EXERCISE

Another possibility when you have a layover is to use the time for some exercise. Most airports have lockers in which you can store your belongings. Stow your suitcase, and take a walk! If the weather permits, you may want to go outside. Air in planes and terminals can get stale, and the fresh air will revitalize you. Men generally wear comfortable shoes, and this is easy for them to do. Increasingly women are wearing comfortable tennis or jogging shoes when they travel. However, many still wear heels, as they struggle to carry their baggage. If you are a woman traveller, get in the habit of carrying your heels and wearing comfortable shoes while you travel. Not only will you feel better, it will save wear and tear on your expensive heels.

Many hotels with exercise rooms and pools are now located adjacent to airports. If you have an extended layover, for a small fee you can use such facilities. To find out if this service is available at an airport you frequent, check with the on-site hotel.

LUGGAGE

There are two views on luggage. On the one hand, if you carry it on, you know for certain it will make it to your destination at the same time you do. This is critical when your baggage carries equipment or supplies essential for your business. In such cases, you are wise to take it with you. Learn to pack light. Take only what you will need. This usually means if you will be gone for a whole week you can wear one suit (men and women) and carry another, along with several shirts or blouses. It is possible to take only one carry-on bag for a full week's business trip. You will find that duffel-type bags provide you with the greatest flexibility and carry the advantage of fitting underneath your seat during those flights on which you can't find overhead space.

The disadvantage of carry-on luggage is the burden, literally, of carrying it. Many veteran travellers have hauled one bag too many, with the result that they have damaged their lower backs. Even a briefcase can feel too heavy when you have back pain. To prevent this, consider a luggage carrier. It is more awkward on the plane and provides another challenge when you're looking for storage space; however, when your connecting flight's gate is halfway across the airport, it can be worth its weight in gold. The other downside to carry-on luggage is storage space. The best way to deal with this is to arrive in plenty of time for the flight, so that as soon as your row number is called, you can board and stow your luggage. If you make many last-minute connections, this is more difficult to do.

The other view on baggage is to check it. Then you don't have to be bothered with carrying it, stowing, or watching it. Without a bag, you are free to board the plane at the last possible moment and therefore will spend the minimum amount of time in the cramped cabin. On the negative side, you will add about 30 minutes to your trip because of the time it takes to claim your baggage when you reach your destination.

Decide which option is best for you based on your physical condition and the nature of your work.

Once on the plane, there are a few guidelines that will help you arrive feeling relaxed and refreshed. First, avoid alcohol and caffeine. Instead, drink mineral water, fruit juice, or herbal tea. Your body is easily dehydrated in the dry atmosphere of the plane, and the fluids will help you feel better.

Second, stretch your body, especially on long flights. Get up and walk around when you can. Every hour or so, roll your shoulders and stretch your arms. Rather than reclining your seat, leave it in the original upright position, which gives you greater back support. Use the reading lights that are provided. Take your shoes off and relax your feet. All these things will help reduce physical fatigue. The takeoff and landing are stressful on the body; you can minimize their effects if you take a walk soon after you arrive at your destination or do something physical to work out the tension.

Plan your trips carefully. Whenever possible, avoid the peak travel times—Sunday through Friday evenings, especially around 5:00 to 6:00 P.M.; Monday mornings; and all day Friday. If you are crossing several time zones, make an effort to arrive early enough to give your body some time to adapt. Order special meals that will be lower in salt, fat, and sugar. Go the day before you are due so you will feel rested and refreshed.

FOOD

Eating on the road can be difficult at best. The restaurant may not be serving when you are hungry, or you may not be able to get the kinds of foods you want. Often, you eat standing or on the run, so that mealtime is not relaxing. The foods, particularly in airports, are high in calories and fat, which causes sluggishness. Consider carrying a small supply of snacks you can eat when a flight has been delayed or when there isn't time to stop between airport and appointment. Fruits such as apples or bananas are easy to carry and easy to eat. Also convenient are nuts or granola bars. Whenever you have a choice, select fruit or a salad at the airport, and you'll notice a positive difference in your energy level. At restaurants, don't hesitate to ask if the chef can prepare something for you that is not on the menu. For example, if the evening special is fried fish, ask to have it broiled. These small steps to exert some control over your diet while you travel can reduce your stress.

If you tire of "hotel food," get a copy of the book *Road Food and Good Food* by Jane and Michael Stern. This book lists restaurants in major cities across the country that serve local or regional specialties. It is a refreshing change from the usual fare.

If possible, choose two or three hotel chains and use them regularly. This way, you reduce some uncertainty by knowing what you can expect. Choose hotels that have some kind of health club facility or proximity to one, so that you can take a swim, sit in the whirlpool or sauna, or work out. Without some form of physical release, the travelling environment is enormously tiring. Also, because it is more difficult to eat healthy foods on the road, exercise can counteract the weight gain many business travelers experience. The other benefit of exercise is that your sleep will be more restful. Many people have difficulty getting a good night's rest in a strange bed in a strange room in a strange city. If you don't sleep well, you start the next morning behind; if this is another day of travel, the sleeplessness is compounded.

SLEEP

If sleeping on the road is problematic for you, another consideration is to carry a small tape recorder and a relaxation tape. This will come in handy not only at bedtime, but also while you are on the plane or in any other waiting situation. If you have a favorite piece of music, carrying it with you can provide a "piece of home away from home."

When you travel, make an extra effort to get a full night's rest. Whether that is 6, 7, or 8 hours will depend on what is normal for you. In other words, travel time is not party time. Do not stay up late going to the local night spots, and do not take a flight that gets you to your destination late at night if you can avoid it.

Do not use alcohol as a sleeping pill. Although it does relax you and can help you fall asleep, alcohol-induced sleep is not as restful. You also may notice that if you have a couple drinks right before going to bed, you tend to awaken earlier. If you are going to drink when you travel, limit it to one drink with dinner, or no drinks if you eat dinner on the plane.

LONELINESS

When you travel, everyone you meet is a stranger, from the gate agent to the flight attendant to the desk clerk to the waitress. This puts you in a situation of perpetual stress, as you are faced with constantly being "on" and constantly selling yourself to get your needs met. There is no one with whom you can let go and relax. You have no comfortable, established rituals with any of these people. Emotional support, discussed in Chapter 5, is rarely available to the business traveller.

There are some ways you can mediate this situation. One is to stay in touch with your friends and family at home. Consider long-distance phone calls one of the costs of doing business. You also can write letters and send post cards to loved ones. This helps you maintain the connection with the significant people in your life. It is also possible to use time on the road to purchase birthday, anniversary, and get-well cards or other small remembrances. These acts bring people closer to you in your mind.

If you know you will make several trips to a particular city, begin to make an investment in some of the people you meet. Look for an opportunity to expand a business association into a friendship.

Then, when you find yourself in town, you can call that person for a "friendly" dinner, not just "business" dinners. You also can make friends with people at the hotel in which you stay, so that when you return you do not feel so much like a stranger.

Many people also find that they feel less needy emotionally when they can create as much normalcy as possible on the road. If you go to movies when you are home, why not go see a movie when you are on the road? If you like to shop when you are home, make an effort to shop some evening when you are on the road. If you enjoy art museums, spend an evening seeing the local one. The more you can maintain your normal activities on the road, the less stress you will feel.

Unfortunately, alcohol becomes the only friend of some people on the road, and before long it can be a problem. Don't let yourself spend your evenings alone in your room with alcohol!

Travelling can be an excellent time to get your work done. In fact, many books and articles have been written on airplanes or waiting in airports. The time on the road is precious, uninterrupted time— no phone calls to disturb you, no drop-in visitors to distract you. Take advantage of this time to write reports, complete correspondence, review trade journals, or plan. You also have time available each evening. Be cautious about seeing clients or customers all day and completing paper work at night, though. This destroys the balance that is so important in managing stress. Give yourself time off, the same as if you were home. Bring a novel or other type of relaxing reading for your evenings.

Make a point of checking in with your office every day or so to keep up with phone calls and items that need your attention. It is worth the time it takes to train your secretary or assistant to process your mail and handle routine matters. In this way, you don't return to a desk piled high with work. You may find that the tape recorder you take for relaxation can also be useful for dictating letters, reports, or memorandums. When you return to the office you aren't faced with loose ends from the trip. If you travel for a full week at a time, you can mail tapes back to the office, so that all your correspondence is ready for your signature when you return.

Get in the habit of completing your expense forms for each trip before you get off the plane at home. Keep all your receipts in one place, so your report is easy to complete. This helps you avoid having to remember expenses from trips you took several weeks ago and helps the company process expense checks in a timely fashion.

SELF-TALK

You're going to be talking to yourself while you're on the road! You want those conversations with yourself to be as positive as possible. You will find the CALM model to be especially helpful in those situations in which things are not going the way you want them to and you feel powerless. At these times, it helps if you accept the situation for what it is rather than invest your energies in anger or worry. If there is a snowstorm and your flight is cancelled,

you aren't going anywhere. Accept reality and relax. In fact, instead of screaming at the gate agent
about your cancelled flight, book a flight in the
morning and go get a hotel room so you can get
some sleep. That's managing stress instead of just
coping with it!

When your room isn't ready, assert yourself, and
then let go of your expectations that everything
should go smoothly. Because one shuttle bus keeps
you waiting 30 minutes, don't overgeneralize that
you "always" have to wait for shuttle buses. Keep
your thoughts positive, and don't attach yourself to
any expectations, beliefs, or feelings. You will travel
more comfortably this way.

Remember, too, your sense of humor. Look for
the light side of your experiences. Ask your cab
driver if he or she has heard anything funny lately.
You'll feel better and live longer if you do.

Even in situations in which it seems you are
powerless and have no control, there still remains
one way in which you always have control. You are
in charge of your reactions. If you react aggressively
or with anger, you will only heighten your stress.
If you respond calmly, maintaining your positive attitude and sense of humor, you will experience less
stress.

SUMMARY

When you travel, take time to plan in advance to
give yourself the advantage of being in control as
much as possible. Travel during off-peak times. Pack
light and carry your luggage unless you have health

problems that prevent you from doing so. Pay attention to what you eat, making a special effort to avoid alcohol and caffeine when you fly. Whenever possible, leave yourself at least one back-up flight in case of cancellations or delays. Arrive at your destination early enough to get a good night's rest. Meet your emotional needs by keeping in touch with loved ones back home or by creating a "normal" life for yourself on the road. Take advantage of opportunities to exercise regularly, whether by walking around the airport or participating in your hotel's fitness club. Finally, pay attention to your thoughts. As long as you are going to talk to yourself, you may just as well keep the conversation positive and upbeat!

9

Terminal Stress: You and Your Computer

Approximately half the workforce currently uses computer monitors or screens. That number is expected to increase as we approach the next century. For many people, automation is turning office work into the newest type of factory work. Not surprisingly, computers are cited ever more frequently as a cause of stress. Although the repetitive work often associated with computers is a psychological stressor for some people, the major stress is physical.

EYESTRAIN

Many workers report suffering from burning, itchy eyes, blurred vision, and eyestrain when they use terminals for extended periods of time. This is a common problem with close work, especially if the work environment is not properly designed.

One major cause of the eyestrain is the screen itself. You want a screen that gives you the ability to control both brightness and contrast. Depending on the time of day, you may need to make adjustments. Also, if anyone else uses the equipment, they may work comfortably with settings different from the ones you select.

The screen also needs to be kept clean. You know how difficult it is to drive with a dirty windshield. It is equally difficult to see a dirty monitor.

The more you can adjust the screen, the more comfortable you will be. You want a screen that tilts and can be turned. A backward tilt of about 10 to 20 degrees makes viewing easier, unless there is a lot of glare in your office, which is worsened when the screen is at this angle. If your screen does not turn, you can buy an inexpensive rotating table to hold it. The screen needs to be placed about 18 inches from your eyes at a height such that the top of the screen is at eye level.

Monitors come with a variety of background and letter colors. You may have experienced "pink eye," a result of viewing green letters on a black background. When you look away after an hour or more, anything white appears pink. This does not hurt your eyes, but does require them to adjust to the colors on the screen. The easiest-to-read combinations are black or dark green screens with yellow or white letters. Color monitors also are easy to read. One caution: If you use a color monitor, don't get too carried away with your color options. Some people suffer eyestrain because of too many colors on the screen. You want a screen that is easy to read and yet restful to the eye.

Another factor in eyestrain is the size and shape of the letters on the screen. Squared letters are easier to read than rounded ones. The letters need to be large enough to read comfortably (3.1 to 4.5 mm) without having to move your head closer to the screen.

Less expensive screens have a low "refresh rate." This is the frequency at which the electron beam that produces the image you see sweeps the screen. If is it less than 65 flashes per second, the letters on your screen may appear to flicker. This, of course, causes more strain on your eyes. If you experiment with your brightness and contrast controls as well as the lighting in the room, you may be able to make the flicker less noticeable. The best solution is to select a screen that has a high enough refresh rate to avoid the problem altogether.

If you wear glasses, particularly bifocals, you may want to consider special glasses for your work at the terminal. Bifocals are not usually designed for the close work you will do at the terminal. Consequently, you may find yourself trying to look up or down at the screen. Either way, after extended periods of time, you will suffer from neck and shoulder strain.

It is a good idea to have your eyes checked at least biannually if you regularly work on the terminal. Some authorities recommend annual checkups. Keep a record of the results so that you can compare them over time.

Ideally, when you work on the terminal you will alternate this close work with other types of work. If you do happen to be spending long stretches of time looking at the screen, periodically look up and allow your eyes to focus on some object that is off in the distance. This gives your eyes a brief break.

There are probably more complaints about glare than any of the other causes of eyestrain. Glare occurs whenever light is reflected off a surface. Screens with antireflection coatings help this problem. Antiglare filters that cover the screens are usually not much help. Although they reduce glare, they also distort the image, causing equal or worse eyestrain. The best way to reduce glare is to change your lighting.

LIGHTING

Whether you have natural light or artificial light, if it is positioned improperly it can create glare on your screen and stress for you. As a general rule, when you work at a monitor, you will need less light than the average office worker. Few offices adjust for this, and as a result you often suffer from overillumination and glare.

If you have a window in your office, you want to position yourself and your terminal so the light comes in from your side. You do not want the light coming in over your back, because it will reflect on the screen and cause glare. Nor do you want the direct sunlight in front of you because then you will strain against it. You will need shades or blinds so that depending on the time of day you can control the amount of natural light that enters your work area.

If you have artificial light in your office, ideally you want a combination of overhead and "task" lighting. The latter is lighting you can control depending on the project you have. For example, you may want low lighting in the office so you can view your screen easily and bright lighting on the source document you are typing. Position your desk between rows of overhead lighting so you don't get unnecessary glare. Whenever possible, have concealed overhead lighting that is reflected from the upper walls, not from your screen.

To further reduce glare, be sure that all the surfaces in your office are matte finish. This includes the desk, the walls, the floors, and the keyboard. If you are uncertain how much glare you have in your office, you can do a quick test by looking at any glossy magazine. If there are any blank spots when you try to look at it, you have glare in your office.

When light reflects off your screen, the natural tendency is to compensate by changing your posture or your position in the chair to try to avoid it. Unfortunately, we trade eyestrain for body pain in the form of sore muscles.

THE CHAIR

The number one cause of absenteeism in the workplace is back pain. Fifty to eighty percent of the population suffers from back pain either sporadically or continuously. A major culprit is the chairs in which we sit.

A chair is among the most important items in your office. There is no such thing as "one size fits all," although that is how most chairs are sold. A poorly fitting chair causes back pain, fatigue, and irritability. It's worth your while to invest some time when you select a chair.

Because there is no such thing as an "average" person, a chair needs to be adjustable. The greater the number of adjustments, the greater the likelihood that you will be comfortable for prolonged periods of sitting. First, the height needs to be adjustable. Ideally your hips and knees will bend at right angles and your feet will rest flat on the floor. Your elbows will also bend 90 degrees to reach the keyboard. For most people, the highest point of the chair seat will be about 2 inches less than the distance between the crease behind your knees and the floor when you are standing.

The seat of the chair needs to be made of a fabric that can "breathe." Otherwise you will find yourself becoming too hot when you sit all day. The fabric also needs to be textured rather than slick, so you don't slide off the chair! Look at the shape of the seat. It needs to be rounded off on the front—that is, *scrolled*—so it doesn't dig into the back of your legs. Also notice the size of the seat. If it is too long from front to back you will put stress on the lower back. A general rule is to have 5 inches behind the crease of your knee and the seat when you are sitting. Less or more than that will strain your musculature.

Your chair also needs a backrest. If you sit for several hours at a time, the backrest needs to be adjustable, and make contact with your back 4 to 6 inches above the seat. A small kidney-shaped backrest that fits snugly into the lower back and tilts back and forth is preferred by most people.

The base of your chair needs five prongs to be stable. Many American chairs have only four prongs. When you move sideways, it is possible for the chair to overturn if it has fewer than five prongs.

A well-designed chair will not help if you do not sit in it properly. Keep your back straight back and pressed up against the backrest for maximum comfort. Lean forward from the waist and hips, not by curling the back. You will experience less back pain if your knees are above your hips. To accomplish this, use a footrest. This is essential if you are short and working on a "standard" desk.

YOUR DESK

Of all office furniture, the desk is usually the least adjustable. This makes an adjustable chair even more critical. If your desk is the proper height, when you work at it your hands and forearms will be at right angles to your body. For most people this requires a desk height of approximately 24 to 28 inches. To achieve this ideal, especially for women, it may be necessary to raise the height of your chair. When you do this, you may suddenly notice your feet are not touching the ground. Then a moveable foot rest becomes essential. You see how we have a case of dominoes here! If one part of the system is off, the body is forced to compensate, which it can do easily for short periods of time. However, if you are working at the terminal for 2 hours or more, your body will not be able to adapt without causing you pain.

A computer keyboard belongs on a special, *lower* table or desk, not on a regular office desk. If you put it on a regular desk, it will be too high, resulting in body strain. Desks designed for computers often have an adjustable drop front so you can customize the height.

Be sure you have enough space under the desk for your thighs and knees, including enough space to have your knees parallel or above your hips.

THE KEYBOARD

The most comfortable keyboards are detached from the screen so you can position them as you want. They are also narrow so that your hands are not required to make a long stretch to reach the keys. Also, look for keyboards that have a slight tilt—about 10 degrees. These are easier on your hands and wrists than flat keyboards.

The QWERTY (the first six letters on the top row of the keyboard) keyboards that we all use are probably here to stay, even though they are not the easiest to use. There have been several proposed alternatives that would require less hand movement and not discriminate as much against the left-handed typist, but with all the keyboards presently in the marketplace, it is highly unlikely we will see any changes soon.

Keep an adjustable document holder near the screen. It will be easiest to read if it is approximately the same height as the screen. This helps you avoid shifting your head from the screen down to a document on the desk. It is also easier on your eyes.

REST BREAKS

As we have said elsewhere in this book, it is important to take frequent rest breaks. In fact, a brief break every hour has been shown to increase productivity. Take 3 to 5 minutes every hour to stretch. At this time, you want to get up, move around and walk if you can. If you need to stay at your desk, then you can do any of the following exercises to refresh your muscles and enable you to continue to work at the terminal with the minimal amount of strain.

You are likely to notice tension in your shoulders and neck. The best way to reduce this is to do the shoulder shrugs and neck rolls described in Chapter 5. In addition, roll your shoulders gently to the front three or four times and then to the back three or four times.

Another energizer for your arms is to extend them straight out to your sides, parallel with the floor, and do arm circles. Start with small circles at first and gradually make them bigger and bigger. Then reverse the direction, once again going from small to big circles.

To ease any soreness you may have in your lower back, take a moment and press your back up against the backrest on the chair. Use your abdominal muscles to do the pressing. Release your back and repeat two more times.

If your legs are feeling stiff, there are several quick and easy exercises you can do. The first is to place both feet together flat on the floor in front of you. Then, lift only your heels off the ground and lower them back to the ground. Do this quickly at least ten times to stimulate the soles of your feet.

Then, lift one leg straight out from the knee and return it to the floor. Repeat this with the other leg.

Continue alternating for at least ten repetitions. In addition to extending the leg, you can rotate your ankle clockwise and counterclockwise before returning your leg to the ground.

You also may want to stand up next to your desk and, resting your hand on the edge of your desk to steady yourself, swing one leg from the hip, first forward and then backward. After eight repetitions, turn and swing the other leg.

You do not need to do all of these exercises at each break. Use the ones that seem most helpful at the time. If you can release physical tension every hour or so, you will discover that you feel less fatigued at the end of the day.

If muscle tension is a problem for you, please reread the section on progressive muscle relaxation in Chapter 5. By learning that technique, you can relax your shoulders and back while you work at the keyboard. Too often we tense muscles unnecessarily. Consequently, we suffer from soreness and fatigue.

Remember, too, to pay attention to your breathing. When we concentrate there is a tendency to hold the breath and breathe more shallowly. This further contributes to the overall tension in the body. Take a moment now for a few slow, relaxing diaphragmatic breaths.

SUMMARY

No doubt the computer is here to stay. To work comfortably with it, you may need to make some adjustments to your individual workstation. Select equipment and position it to minimize eyestrain. Have your eyes checked on a regular basis, and if you wear glasses, check with your ophthalmologist about special lenses for working with the screen. Also, pay attention to the lighting in your office and try to reduce glare, a major cause of fatigue and eyestrain. The comfort of your chair is critical when you work at the terminal for extended periods of time. You want one with as many adjustments as possible, minimally for height and the backrest. Adjust your chair to the desk, which is rarely adjustable, and get a footrest if necessary. Remember that you will need stretch breaks at least once an hour to keep you fresh and productive.

10

It Was the Best of Times, It Was the Worst of Times: Organizational Change

Organizational change . . . no company is immune to it. We all face it to varying degrees. The late 1980s brought an epidemic of corporate takeovers, mergers and buy outs that left shock waves months and years after the events. A global marketplace has changed how and where goods are manufactured. Consequently, manufacturing companies have faced plant reductions and plant closings. To stay competitive requires new technology, which has an impact on the work force, sometimes shrinking it, often changing duties and responsibilities. All these changes have impact on employees who need to adapt, adjust, cope, and respond. Often, this is stressful.

CHANGE CAUSES STRESS

Change is closely linked to stress for many reasons. First, change involves loss. Whenever there is something new (a person, technology, structure, process, and so on), it alters and sometimes replaces the old and familiar. For most of us, what is known is comfortable and easier to cope with than the unknown. The second reason, then, that we feel stress during times of change is that change brings uncertainty. Uncertainty is accompanied by a feeling of loss of control, and we know that control is directly related to the amount of stress we feel. Third, any change requires an adjustment period. We need to learn new ways of doing things or how to interact with new people or integrate new values and beliefs about the work. These adjustments take time and place demands on us.

Although change is associated with stress, it is not change per se that is causing us distress. It is the *rate* of change and the volume of changes that are the true culprits. Today it happens so fast we have trouble keeping up with it. Information is doubling every 20 months. Our technology compounds this with the increasing numbers of products that allow things to happen faster and faster. Even overnight mail services are slow since the introduction of the fax machine.

Control becomes a key word as we strive to manage change. When we choose the changes for ourselves we feel differently about them than when the changes are imposed on us. Ken and Warren are both in new supervisory jobs. Ken is thrilled and looks forward to all the new things he has to learn. Warren, on the other hand, feels depressed and dreads going into work in the morning. Why the difference? Isn't everyone thrilled when they get a new job? No. Ken had been preparing to become a supervisor for a year, taking the presupervisory training courses, learning from his boss, and reading in his spare time about effective supervision. Warren had been a manager with his company for 4 years. After several quarters of slow sales, the company decided to reduce their management ranks and demoted Warren to a supervisory position. Warren felt powerless in his situation and consequently experienced some stress symptoms. Ken experienced no negative symptoms of stress around his change because he initiated the change.

RESPONDING TO CHANGE

The reality of most organizational change is that we are not its architects. It is designed and executed by higher levels of management or outside forces. We are faced with responding and coping. Most of us respond in one or some combination of these ways: denial, sabotage, information gathering, resistance, and excitement. Imagine that your company has just decided to computerize its operations. In the last several months, hundreds of PCs have been pur-chased and put on everyone's desk, from the secre-tary's to the President's. If you conduct some research, you will probably see these reactions.

Denial

Some people will cope with the change by pretend-ing it has not occurred. They will continue to act as if everything is the same as it always has been. For example, when Robbie got her new office com-puter, she would not allow the company to remove her typewriter. She explained that she would still need it for certain forms that were not easily com-pleted using the PC. The company agreed. However, her boss noticed a week later that Robbie was using the typewriter for all her work and was not using the computer at all. He spoke with her about it, and she gave more reasons why the computer was a great tool for other people but was not suitable for her work. It took removing her typewriter before Robbie accepted that she needed to learn to use the new equipment.

Sabotage

Occasionally someone feels so distressed by the changes or so opposed to them that they sabotage the change effort. Stewart was asked to change from manually maintaining the company's books to put-ting them on a computer. He was intimidated by the computer and thought it was a bad idea to automate. Stewart continually put the wrong data into the computer so that the reports he produced were useless to the company. Worse, he "accidentally" erased data more than once from the hard disk when he had no backup copies. When the company finally noticed the consultant's bills for fixing Stewart's errors, they decided it was time to talk to him about how he was handling the change.

Information Gathering

When faced with a change, some people respond by collecting as much information as possible to help them cope. When Helen learned the company was going to automate, the first thing she did was go to her boss and ask exactly what kind of computer she was getting. Then she went to the nearest computer store to look at it and talk to the salesman about it. She took home all the literature and read it carefully. Within a week, she went to her boss to find out about computer courses. Excited to see Helen's reaction, Marsha arranged for Helen to take an introductory course. Helen loved the course and asked her instructor what books she could read to help her better understand her new computer. She followed up on his recommendations, and when her computer arrived she felt she was seeing an old friend. The more she prepared herself with information, the easier it was for her to accept the change. Gathering information was the way in which Helen maintained control over the change.

Resistance

Sometimes people simply do not like or do not agree with a proposed change. Sometimes they are afraid of the change or feel it conflicts with their values. In these situations, they may try to prevent the change from being implemented. That's what Kathy did. Her computer arrived, and a day or so later she received a schedule for computer training. She called the instructor and requested to be changed to a different class because her schedule was "too busy." This happened again and again until everyone around her was trained and using the computers. When her boss asked her to produce something with the word processing program, she would explain that because she hadn't had the training yet, it would take too long to use the computer. Kathy was always warm and friendly when approached about the computer, so it took about 6 weeks before her boss realized she was resisting converting to the new system.

Excitement

Some people look forward to change, even though it may be imposed from the outside. It is their perceptions and attitudes that enable them to embrace change instead of fighting it. Robert was excited when he learned that he would be working with the computer. He waited in anticipation until they were delivered and was anxious to turn his on and see what it could do. His kids had been learning about computers in school, and he felt lost when they talked about them. His wife used one where she worked, and Robert felt left out of their discussions. Now he, too, could talk about computers at the dinner table. Robert signed up for all the training courses, and was patient when at first it took him longer with the computer than without it. For several Saturdays he came into the office to practice using it, until in just a few weeks he was comfortable and proficient.

Some changes take more time to implement than others. They often become sources of sneaking stress, discussed in Chapter 1. Mergers, acquisitions, and buy outs are examples of this kind of change, often taking from 1 to 2 years to complete. Read on to see how one company got through this process.

BUY OUTS, MERGERS, AND ACQUISITIONS

Lauren worked in the payroll department of a Fortune 500 company. Every morning when she turned on the computer a message greeted her with the date, temperature, and price of the company's stock. She'd been with the company 8 years and the stock had been flat for the last 3 of those years. So, she watched with interest as the stock began a gradual ascent. Being curious she asked questions about what the company was doing to increase the value of the stock. No one could explain it. Then it began to dawn on her—someone was buying the company stock, perhaps in preparation for a corporate takeover.

A month later there was a story in the *Wall Street Journal*. Someone was accumulating stock for a hostile takeover. Five floors up, senior management read the stories in shock. Mark, Vice President of Operations, became a key player in the events that took place over the next 9 months. For him, it was a challenging and agonizing nine months during which he gained 15 pounds and took up smoking again.

After Mark and the other Vice Presidents recovered from their shock, they began their planning. How would they respond to this offer to buy them out? It took them weeks to put together a leveraged buyout package that they thought would work. These weeks were filled with long hours, difficult decisions, secrecy, and isolation.

Downstairs Lauren and her colleagues were frustrated and confused. Productivity slipped as people spent their days feeding the rumor mill with speculations from "It's all a big joke" to "We will all lose our jobs." No one seemed able to provide them with any answers. When Lauren asked her manager what was happening, her manager said she didn't know. Convinced management was holding back, she approached senior management in the elevator. Their expressionless statement was "no comment." Lauren felt powerless. She didn't know whether to look for another job or wait for things to blow over. She tried to keep a positive attitude by talking with friends and her husband, but some days she just didn't feel like coming to work. She also noticed a dull ache in her stomach that never seemed to go away.

After months of uncertainty, management made their announcement. They would fight the takeover with an attempt to buy back the company. Everyone cheered! For a few weeks there was cautious optimism as people held out the hope that management could work a miracle. However, then there was another blow. Buying back the company couldn't be done without a significant downsizing.

Finally, the company's version of Black Monday came and layoff notices were given. A company went into mourning as friends said good-bye to each other. Some people stayed in their old jobs, some stayed with the company in "new" positions, and others, with the assistance of outplacement, went off to seek a new future.

Let's take a closer look at what this situation can tell us about the change process in an organization.

First, we see that people at all levels of the organization feel apprehension. This is normal because change brings with it loss, uncertainty, an adjustment period, and disrupted relationships. Consequently, change often is accompanied by feelings of stress. The stress is even greater when you feel powerless. Mark felt a different kind of stress than Lauren did. He was an active participant in the planning process that resulted in the leveraged buy out. He experienced some feelings of control and power over his destiny. Lauren, on the other hand, did not know what was being done, was subjected to rumors with no basis in fact, and felt powerless in her efforts to find out information that would have a direct impact on her future and her well-being. She had much less control.

What Mark knew helped him gain some sense of control, and yet he was unable to share what he knew with anyone because of the delicacy of the situation. This created a painful conflict of values for him, because he had tried to create a corporate culture of openness and two-way communication, yet now he was withholding information he knew his people wanted. Unable to share what he knew, he withdrew from his usual support resources and felt more alone and isolated than ever before. He ate to soothe himself and took up smoking again.

The change process disrupted relationships at several different levels. The trust that had been developed between senior management and the rest of the company was eroded during the months of secrecy. Employees began to feel they could not believe what they were told. With the layoffs, some departments were merged with others and some were abolished altogether. When it was all "over," the survivors were faced with developing new relationships to get the job done.

The organization for which you work will undoubtedly face changes. This is essential for it to stay vital and alive. Change stimulates us to keep growing and developing. If we aren't growing, then we are dying. There is no such thing as standing still. The changes will be accompanied by some stress. The degree of stress will be based on the amount of control you feel over the change and whether or not it is a change you want or believe in.

CHANGE AND THE CALM MODEL

Lauren and Mark went through a process that has been experienced by hundreds of thousands of employees across the country. How people in their company coped is typical of how people in other companies have responded to massive organizational change.

To help yourself during organizational change, keep these things in mind. The only way you can have enough information to change the situation is to *ask questions*. The rumor mill is often wrong and can create unnecessary anxiety. Be prepared: You may be told, "I don't know." When the company is undergoing major changes, as in mergers and buy outs, they need to keep their strategy secret from the press and outsiders. They know that a secret is a heavy burden to carry, and most people under stress do confide in someone. They can't afford to take the risk of revealing their strategy until they are prepared for everyone to know it. Nonetheless, you can continue to ask; you never know when the people you ask will be able to answer.

There will be things you cannot change. Accept the situation for what it is and *maintain a positive attitude*. This is not the time for shoulds, mental filters, overgeneralizations, or any of the other negative thoughts we discussed in Chapter 3. Stay in the present as much as possible instead of jumping ahead 6 months and worrying about what will happen then. Remember that in every threatening situation there is opportunity. Look for what good can come out of the change, and don't focus on the negative outcomes. Lauren and Mark will both now say that the company is more efficient than it ever was. Yes, it was a painful experience, and yes, it was unfortunate to lose so many good employees. Yet, the company has benefited from the difficult experience.

It is in difficult and challenging situations that we can sometimes become more than we are. Don't add to the organizational stress with a negative attitude.

Let go of your expectations that things will happen fast. When your organization goes through change, the process will occur in steps rather than all at once. This can be frustrating, because you want to move through the discomfort and uncertainty as quickly as possible. It takes time. The bigger the organization, the slower the process. Going through change is like threading a needle. The organization is analogous to a piece of thread, and the eye of the needle is analogous to the change process. A small organization gets through the process like a piece of thread through the eye of a needle. A larger organization is like threading yarn through a needle: Sometimes it unravels a little before you can get it through. Remember, too, that some people will "pass through the eye" sooner than others. Top management may be in the final stages of accepting the changes when lower management is first being informed.

Manage your lifestyle. Take care of yourself physically and emotionally during the process, and as much as you can, make it fun.

Celebrate! As you complete parts of the change process, give yourself time to acknowledge your accomplishments. Organizational change is hard work. Damon worked for a consulting firm that assisted major corporations in the automation of their manufacturing, inventory, and warehousing operations. These projects generally required 3 to 4 years to implement. He learned that a key to managing stress and keeping morale positive was to divide the project into a series of subprojects. These were monitored on a big board that everyone could see.

When they met one of their deadlines, there was cheering, a big dinner, a recounting of their trials and tribulations, and a recommitment to the next phase. Damon recognized that 3 years is too long for most of us to wait for any recognition of our efforts.

You will need people who can listen to you and provide the emotional support we described in Chapter 5. Listening to the rumor mill is different from support. You also may need the informational support that others who have been through a similar situation can provide. Sometimes this support can result in mutually beneficial partnerships. This happened in Lauren's department. When the time for layoffs came, her department was hit hard; almost half of the department had to leave. One man who was asked to stay had been thinking of relocating to another state. The company offered a liberal severance package, which he saw as an excellent cushion for the time he would spend job hunting. One of his colleagues who wanted to stay in the area and stay with the company had been given her notice. They talked and agreed between themselves to trade places. Their boss was agreeable when they went in to discuss it with him. Each of them ended up happy with the situation. This kind of ongoing communication allowed them each to have greater control over the situation and create a win-win outcome for each other and the company.

SUMMARY

In summary, if you work in an organization, you can anticipate that you will undergo organizational change at some point in time. It is difficult and creates stress for us because of the loss we feel, the period of uncertainty and adjustment, and the disrupted relationships. When we have been a part of creating the change or when it is a change we favor, the coping is easier because we feel more control than when it is imposed. In any change process we may respond with denial, sabotage, resistance, information gathering, or excitement. Ultimately we will need to accept the changes. Such acceptance is easier if we ask questions along the way, keep positive attitudes, celebrate our successes, take small steps, and maintain a support system.

In Conclusion

Congratulations! By reading this book you have taken the first step toward managing stress. You have increased your awareness and understanding of it. Now you know that nearly all stress—aside from environmental stressors like noise and pollution—comes from our perceptions, thoughts, and beliefs. We do it to ourselves!

Despite all the demands, pressures, and changes in our lives, we can exert some control over the stress we experience. We can choose to CALM down. We can choose a lifestyle that will minimize rather than exacerbate the stressors in our life.

Remember, when you first notice yourself feeling stress, stop and remind yourself you can CALM down. Ask yourself, "Is there any way I can *change the situation* to reduce the stress I am feeling?" If the answer is "yes," take action! If the answer is "no," then *accept what can't be changed* without adding emotional upset to your stress. *Let go* of ir-rational beliefs that-upset you. *Let go* of behaviors that threaten your health. Then invest your energy in prevention by choosing to *manage your lifestyle* for health and wellness. Pay attention to what you eat, exercise regularly, take time to relax and don't hesitate to use your support systems.

If you follow this simple prescription you'll have stress on your side! But don't be fooled into think-ing that because it is simple, it is easy. Knowing *how* to CALM down is not the same as *implementing* what you know. This book has given you all the tools and told you what you can do. Now you need to make the lifestyle changes that will put you in con-trol of your stress. I know you can do it! Good luck!

Bibliography

Adams, Ramona Shepherd, Herbert A. Otto, and AuDeane Shepherd Cowley. *Letting Go: Uncomplicating Your Life.* New York: MacMillan Publishing Co., 1980.

Beale, Lucy, and Rick Fields. *The Win Win Way.* San Diego, Calif.: Harcourt Brace Jovanovich, 1987.

Berne, Eric. *Games People Play.* New York: Grove Press, Inc., 1964.

Bramson, Robert M. *Coping with Difficult People.* Garden City, N.Y.: Anchor Press/Doubleday, 1981.

Briggs, Dorothy Corkille. *Celebrate Your Self.* Garden City, N.Y.: Doubleday and Company, Inc., 1971.

Bristol, Claude M. *The Magic of Believing.* Englewood Cliffs, N.J.: Prentice-Hall, Inc., 1976.

Burley-Allen, Madelyn. *Managing Assertively.* New York: John Wiley and Sons, Inc., 1983.

Burns, David D. *Feeling Good.* New York: Morrow, 1980.

Campbell, Joseph. *The Power of Myth.* New York: Doubleday, 1988.

Charlesworth, Edward A., and Ronald G. Nathan. *Stress Management.* New York: Ballantine Books, 1982.

Cousins, Norman. *Anatony of an Illness.* New York: Norton, 1979.

Crum, Thomas F. *The Magic of Conflict.* New York: Simon and Schuster, 1987.

Ellis, Albert. *A New Guide to Rational Living.* Englewood Cliffs, N.J.: 1975.

Faelten, Sharon, David Diamond, and the Editors of Prevention Magazine. *Take Control of Your Life.* Emmaus, Pa.: Rodale Press, 1988.

Ferguson, Marilyn. *The Aquarian Conspiracy.* Los Angeles, Calif.: J.P. Tarcher, Inc., 1980.

Forbes, Rosalinda. *Corporate Stress.* Garden City, N.Y.: Doubleday and Company, Inc., 1979.

Frankl, Viktor E. *Man's Search for Meaning.* New York: Washington Square Press, 1959.

Friedman, Meyer, and Diane Ulmer. *Treating Type A Behavior — and Your Heart.* New York, 1984.

Fritz, Robert. *The Path of Least Resistance.* Salem, Mass.: DMA, Inc., 1984.

Glasser, William. *Reality Therapy.* New York: Harper and Row, 1975.

Hanson, Peter G. *The Joy of Stress.* Kansas City, Mo.: Andrews, McMeel and Parker, 1985.

Hill, Napoleon. *Think and Grow Rich.* North Hollywood, Calif.: Wilshire Book Company, 1966.

Jaffe, Dennis T., and Cynthia D. Scott. *Take This Job and Love It.* New York: Simon and Schuster, Inc., 1988.

James, Jennifer. *Success Is the Quality of Your Journey.* New York: Newmarket Press, 1983.

Jamison, Kaleel. *The Nibble Theory and the Kernel of Power.* New York: Paulist Press, 1984.

Kanter, Rosabeth Moss. *The Change Masters.* New York: Simon and Schuster, 1983.

Liebman, Shelley. *Do It at Your Desk.* New York: Tilden Press, 1982.

Makower, Joel. *Office Hazards.* Washington, D.C.: Tilden Press, 1981.

Maltz, Maxwell. *Psycho-Cybernetics.* New York: Simon and Schuster, 1960.

Manning, George, and Kent Curtis. *Stress without Distress.* Cincinnati, Ohio: South-Western Publishing Company, 1988.

Matteson, Michael T. and John M. Ivancevich. *Controlling Work Stress.* San Francisco, Calif.: Jossey-Bass Publishers, 1987.

McQuade, Walter, and Ann Aikman. *Stress.* Toronto, Canada: Bantam Books, 1974.

Mills, James W. *Coping with Stress: A Guide to Living.* New York: John Wiley and Sons, Inc., 1982.

Mitchell, Margaret. *Gone with the Wind.* New York: Macmillan, 1936.

Moskowitz, Robert. *How to Organize Your Work and Your Life.* Garden City, N.Y.: Doubleday and Company, Inc., 1981.

Pelletier, Kenneth R. *Healthy People in Unhealthy Places.* New York: Delacorte Press/Seymour Lawrence, 1982.

Pritchett, Price, and Ron Pound. *Business as Unusual.* Dallas, Tex.: Pritchett and Associates, Inc., 1988.

Pritchett, Price. *The Employee Survival Guide to Mergers and Acquisitions.* Dallas, Tex.: Pritchett and Associates, Inc., 1987.

Rowan, Roy. *The Intuitive Manager.* Boston: Little, Brown and Company, 1986.

Schucman, Helen. *A Course in Miracles.* Tiburon, Calif.: Foundation for Inner Peace, 1975.

Sehnert, Keith W. *Stress/Unstress.* Minneapolis, Minn.: Augsburg Publishing House, 1981.

Seyle, Hans, *The Stress of Life.* rev.ed. New York: McGraw-Hill, Inc., 1976.

Shaffer, Martin. *Life after Stress.* New York, New York: Plenum Press, 1982.

Siegel, Bernie S. *Love, Medicine and Miracles.* New York: Harper and Row, 1986.

Stellman, Jeanne Mager. *Office Work Can Be Dangerous to Your Health.* New York: Pantheon Books, 1983.

Stern, Jane, and Michael Stern. *Road Food and Good Food.* New York: Alfred A. Knopf, Inc., 1986.

Storr, Anthony. *Solitude.* New York: The Press Press, 1988.

Stroebel, Charles F. *QR: The Quieting Reflex.* New York: G.P. Putnam's Sons, 1982.

Tubesing, Nancy Loving, and Donald A. Tubesing. *Structured Exercises in Stress Management.* Duluth, Minn.: Whole Person Press, 1984.

"Video Display Terminals . . . The Human Factor," *National Safety Council.* Chicago, Ill.: 1982.

Yankelovich, Daniel. *New Rules.* New York: Random House, 1981.

Warshaw, Leon J. *Managing Stress.* Reading, Mass.: Addison-Wesley Publishing Company, 1979.

Yates, Jere E. *Managing Stress.* New York: Amacom, 1979.

Index